AN ESSAY
ON
HINDUISM

AN ESSAY ON HINDUISM: ITS FORMATION AND FUTURE

SHRIDHAR VENKATESH KETKAR

GYAN

Published by

Gyan Publishing House
5, Ansari Road
Daryaganj, New Delhi-110002
Phone: 011-47034999, 9811692060
E-mail: books@gyanbooks.com

Distribution Network
gyanbooks.com
India, USA, Canada, UK, Australia

ISBN: 978-93-7014-083-7 (PB)

First Published, 1911

2nd Impression 2025

Printed at: Gyan Press, Delhi.

AN ESSAY ON HINDUISM
Author: SHRIDHAR VENKATESH KETKAR

AN ESSAY ON HINDUISM

AN ESSAY ON HINDUISM

ITS FORMATION AND FUTURE

Illustrating the Laws of Social Evolution as reflected in the History of the Formation of Hindu Community

By

SHRIDHAR V. KETKAR, M.A., Ph.D

Doctor of Philosophy in Sociology, Politics, and Political Economy.
The ex-President of the Society of Comparative Theology and Philosophy, Cornell University, U.S.A.

SECOND VOLUME OF
"HISTORY OF CASTE IN INDIA"

LONDON
LUZAC AND CO
46, GREAT RUSSELL STREET, W.C
1911

INTRODUCTION

VERY often a question is asked, " What is the relation of caste system to Hindu religion ? " A question like this is easy enough to ask, but very difficult to answer. The difficulty is not due to the incomprehensibility of the phenomena themselves but to the false ideas which exist as a result of the present currency of a wrong system of thought. The study of social science in Europe is new, and new as it is, it has received a very one-sided development. The students of social sciences had not a good knowledge of civilizations other than occidental. Moreover, their ideas have been fettered by the limitations of their own languages, and this fact prevented them from studying their own civilization in a manner sufficiently objective. In order to answer the above question properly it would be necessary to correct radical misconceptions and to modify terminologies and classifications. An occidental reader is to be carried into a presentation of entirely different social phenomena, which are to be explained to him in a language not very well suited to interpret them.

In order to answer the above question, it is necessary to lay down principles of the scientific study of religions, yet crudely developed. I am also compelled to make a digression in logic and method in order to justify my departure from existing usage and my propagations of new terms and distinctions. More than this. In order to explain the formation and structure of Hinduism I had to introduce some theories regarding the march of civilization, social organization and organization of thought. In doing so, I had to accept the burden of giving proofs for the theory. Such a multiplicity of inquiries would necessarily cause some irregularity in the presentation of thought.

I think no historian before me has been so unfortunate in his choice of the subject. The development of Hindu society is a subject which has very few parallels as far as instruction is concerned, but a history of it offers by no means the most pleasant reading. The subject is made much more repulsive by imagination, and the name of the subject itself is such as would induce an average reader to fly from the book. In a History of Caste, the writer ha no opportunity of dwelling on personalities. He has no series of campaigns to describe and no interesting stories to tell. In writing this history for a period extending over several millenniums, a large number of questions of scientific interest are to be discussed, and the inquirer has often to lay down the subject in hand and to master a number of sciences and to treat purely scientific questions which may have bearing on the History of Caste, leaving all other things aside.

But the difficulties do not end here. Generally, the task of investigation and that of narration is considerably divided. A historian is not asked to take part in discussions connected with various anthropological sciences. Most of the historians do not need to go deep in various controversies; but the practical aim which the writer has in view prevents him from shunning the part either of the investigator or of the narrator. He has to do more; he has to be on guard not to tire the reader by his controversies, which, however necessary they may be to the scientific world, are of no great interest to an average reader. He has also to take care that his readers may not charge him with a desire to display learning, an impression which is very likely to arise in the mind of a reader.

This work is being published in parts. Each volume is published as soon as it is prepared and under this condition it is inevitable that I may discover some mistake or change my opinion after the publication of the volume. Under these conditions if I change my opinion I should not be charged with inconsistency provided I call attention to the change.

Religion and Constitution.—Whether the caste system is allowed by the Hindu religion or not is a vain question. Occidental peoples ask it and answer it also, in their own way. The Hindus also take the question as it is and put before themselves, without considering the rationality of the question. The Europeans ask this question simply because it is rational with reference to their own society, and because they cannot imagine a society of any other kind. Their own society was formed on pre-existing constitution. A certain master and his teaching existed and those who joined the theophratry and followed its teachings became members of the tribe. The members undertook to follow the teachings as they are. Thus it became an important matter for every person to find out whether any particular dogma or doctrine can be found in the religion, that is, in the original constitution which he is supposed to follow. If anything is approved of by the master it is to be followed; if it is disapproved, it should be abandoned. In this case whether anything is allowed by religion or not is a perfectly natural inquiry just as the members of the legislatures of the United States, while voting for any law, would consider whether the particular procedure is allowed by Constitution.

Religion and Occidental Politics.—The western world became members of the theophratry of Christ, and the principles and traditions of this theophratry became the common law of Europe. The King, like every other man, was required to follow religion, and subjects were expected to obey the king if the latter follows the religion. As all European princes who called themselves Christians were supposed to follow the principles of their religion in their government, Christian religion became the fundamental law of life and State. The execution of this fundamental law was carried through the organization called Church. A King was to follow religion as interpreted by the Church. Thus political law became subordinated to the Church.

The result of this ideal was that all the Christian countries of Western Europe became subject to Rome. Though subjection to Church is logical outcome of the doctrines held, many countries did not like the idea of being subject to Church. It is an unfortunate irony of fate that our feelings do not always coincide with our ideas, and this lack of coincidence makes our lives inconsistent. Very often a doctrine is attacked not on account of the simple hunger for truth or desire for consistency but on account of the fact that the doctrine hurts our sentiments.

A state could assert its independence against the Catholic Church in three ways. They are :

(i) To recognize the supremacy of religion in life, and to accept the interpretation of Church as authority but to denounce the traditional head of the Church.

(ii) To denounce Church as the interpreter of religion,

and assume the right of individual interpretation, but to recognize the supremacy of religion itself.

(iii) To deny the supremacy of religion as a prime determinant of laws, manners, life, etc.

The first process asks neither for individual interpretation, nor for the independence of politics against religion, but only demands a division in the Church to remove the subjection of a State or political unit to an organization whose head stays somewhere beyond the confines of the State.

The second process admits the superiority of religion to politics, but does not admit the Church as the interpreter of religion.

Independence of State against the claims of religion could be achieved only by the third process.

These three steps are not merely alternatives. They show the order of development.

Histories of various countries in Europe dealing with the secularization of politics, show that the course of events roughly corresponded with the three stages named above. There is also a good reason for such a sequence. Prior to the rebellion of various countries against the See of Rome, the morals of the people were guided by the instruction of the Church. Such a process is natural when there is no rival social or moral philosophy, and no inductive thought and speculation regarding morals specially by lay classes in the community. The idea of the people was not to seek morals for their own sake but only for the purpose of going to heaven, which could be done only by leading not moral life but a Christian life. The Christian Scriptures again are not a positive treatise on morals, but consist of various books of different character, containing history (mythology), proverbs, legends, gospels, etc. These various books are hardly expected to be consistent. Even in the case of the gospels, there are several contradictions. One peculiarity in the life of teachers like Jesus has been that they were not producers of any systematic philosophy, but men with some good ideas, stray and unorganized, which they taught to the people. The Scriptures being so multiform, it was very difficult to follow them with profit. The task of giving the people such rules for guidance as they could understand fell on the Church. The Church and the priesthood had to create rules for guidance, distinctions between right and wrong, and to explain the Scriptures in such a manner that the people may not lose faith. All this created a strong Catholic tradition, and the greater part of this tradition had been valuable. For example monogamy is not insisted on by the Christian religion, but its inclusion in the Christian life is a contribution by Catholicism.

Acceptance of the interpretation of the Church was the best possible thing for any people who believe in religion, and do not have a rival system of philosophy to enable them to decide between good and bad. Dependence on a book like the Bible would not help anybody to lead a good life, when that person is unaided by any philosophy.

It should not be forgotten that the leaders of the schism at this time were not advocates of tolerance and individual interpretation, but advocates of their own interpretations. Some heretics were more intolerant than the orthodoxy itself. Thus when the nations first wanted to assert their independence of the Catholic theophratry, they could ignore neither the idea that Christian religion is the supreme law, nor the doctrine of submission to the authoritative interpretation of the Church. All that they wanted to create was a national Church authority and to deny the existence of the international Church authority.

Religion and Absolutism.—It should also be remembered that by the time when the Reformation came, the European countries had absolute monarchy. When a country is governed by a monarch free to change or set aside laws and methods of procedure at will, supremacy of the State over Church and the denial of religion as a law at the foundation of society means an encouragement to absolutism and is therefore a very dangerous doctrine either to preach or to assert. The King could not set aside religion himself. For no monarch is strong enough to declare that he is above all laws and rules of morals.

For a King to call himself the head of a Church does not become a very bad declaration, for he thereby does not disown the supremacy of religion but only declares himself to be its administrator.

Religion and Individual Interpretation.—When the Protestants became independent of the See of Rome, they had certain doctrines, differing from those of the Catholic Church. The Bible was sacred to both sects, but that is no reason why two people should believe the same. It is said of the Bible with a certain amount of truth that if one wants to find support to any doctrine one can find it in the Bible ; if one wants to find just the opposite doctrine one can find it in the same book. When the authority of the Pope to interpret the Bible is once denied then there is no limit to the interpreters and interpretations. Some time or other the stage of the right to individual interpretation of the Bible comes.

When there are a large number of societies observing different rules regarding conduct, all deduced from the statements in the Bible but interpreted differently, the natural result is that the country would lose homogeneity and attain diversity. Diversity of conduct and life are of greatest disadvantage to the national life. The danger arising from this diversity would have been great had not popular government and the philosophy of nationalism made their appearance. But before these two came the differences in religious belief had made no little mischief.

Complete Secularization of Politics.—It is the Americans who have realized earlier than any other people that the proper bases for society are not theological but purely political and territorial. Thus the Americans with the foundation of the republic have laid a foundation to the first really political society. America is often called a Christian country, and many Americans ignorantly believe that. It is in fact a higher type of society than the Christian society. Religious belief counts far less in America than anywhere else in the world. They have denied to religion the privilege of being the prime determinant of social growth.

When the people of the United States drew up their Constitution, they made a wonderful departure; they created a society on entirely new lines. The framing of the Constitution of the United States forms a new era in the history of the world. The United States has been the first really political society. The idea of constructing a society under a political constitution has been the most substantial blow rendered to the idea of religion-society. The Constitution of the United States as it is has many defects and many of the principles of Constitution are changed in practice, but this fact should not induce us to disrespect the great work. The important thing in it is not a particular tenet, but the idea of governing society by a written Constitution, when there is no State religion, and no compulsion for the legislators to conform to any set of principles, and to put in the Constitution the principle of toleration.[1] The conduct of the states in the Union, though free to make their own laws, is perfectly in harmony with tradition. No religion is taught in the public schools and colleges and the judiciary of an important and progressive state in the middle West declared the Bible to be sectarian and forbade its use in public schools.

Religion, Constitution and Dharma.—To a society it becomes necessary that there should be some supreme rules either in the shape of laws or morality whose authority would be greater than that of the orders of the government, and to which the latter should be subjected. In a country which may be ruled by a King it is necessary not only to put a certain check to his autocratic power, but that his ordinances should be according to certain principles of conduct roughly called "justice."

In Christendom the King was expected to keep his conduct according to the Christian religion. The Mohamedan kings are supposed to make their laws in accordance with the Mohamedan religion. Under Hinduism, the King is supposed to let his conduct be according to the principles of dharma. The King could not make or unmake dharma.

The only similarity which "dharma" and a "religion" have is in this. Both of them supply the rules to which the other social laws are subordinated.

[1] The only theological tinges which the American Constitution and tradition have are: They require the President to believe in God. They again have Christian holidays like Christmas, Easter, and a national holiday of theological character, i.e., the Thanksgiving Day.

Dharma in India had been indefinite. Christian religion had been unhealthy to political society. But both of these defects are removed in the idea of a written political Constitution.

Under the question as to the supremacy of Church or State lies a question whether the common doctrine and common discipleship or the political allegiance is to be the former of the social groups. The Christian people in the old world yet form entirely an ecclesiastical society. There is State religion. This is a survival or a relic of the past ideal of State. It was formerly regarded in Europe that Christian religion is at the foundation of every State. Every king was required to be Christian, and he was not supposed to issue any ordinance that may be opposed to Christian religion. So Christian religion was supposed to be above all laws. Christian religion is the constitution, the supreme law of the Christian State.

A new order of things resulted from the knowledge that the requirements of any theophratry are not the best basis to be at the foundation of the State. This fact was realized by America earlier than by any other country, and she gave birth to the era of Constitutions. In my opinion those persons who started the idea of Constitution in America deserve at least the same respect which the world gives to men like Gautama, Jesus or Mohamed. I am afraid that even Americans will not agree with me in my estimation of the sages of their revolution, but it will be so because the world is in the habit of venerating men who are thousands of years old.

Hindu method of appealing to Tradition.—Thus, in short, the question whether caste system is permitted by the Hindu religion should not be allowed to be asked at all.

Those who would ask this question and those who would answer in the positive or negative will show nothing but ignorance. When the Hindus of orthodox education ask a question regarding the propriety of a particular custom they inquire whether that custom is :—

(i) Shāstrokta, or Shāstra-sammata, that is mentioned (approvingly) by the sciences (shāstras), or approved of by the sciences.

(ii) Vedokta, mentioned in the Vedas; or

(iii) Purāṇokta, mentioned in the Purāṇas.

The idea involved in the question is that if a custom or a conduct has backing of any of these three, then it is a good custom to be followed. All that a person is expected to do is that he should go by a path by which the good people have gone. Shāstras, Vedas and Purāṇas are all authority to a certain extent. When a recent order was issued by the sacred college (matha) of Sankeshvara His Holiness stated that the particular custom in question has no support of *shruti*, *smriti* and *Purāṇas*. Moreover the phrase *shrutismritipuranokta* is one of frequent occurrence in the ritual.

The goodness of any conduct has been in proportion to the support which it may have from Vedas, sciences and antiquities. If any custom has the support of all these three then the custom deserves the greatest respect. If it has no support of either Vedas or Purananas, and if it is injurious (that is, has no support of Shāstras) then the custom should be abandoned. There were of course people who would say that the authority of the Vedas is supreme, and what is against the Vedas should be abolished; there were also men who advocated the cause of Shāstras. But in general the questions of this nature as to what is the final test of conduct or good or justice was not settled. No single test of the kind was uncompromisingly imposed on the society. The ideal of most general acceptance among the Brahmaṇas was that the conduct should be conformed to sciences. This is the one which they were following in practice. When any person would come for advice they would consult the sciences and not the Vedas. But even there the claims of a single science were not brought forward. The thought had reached so far; the further progress of sciences and philosophy was arrested by the foreign invasion.

Every Hindu is advised to follow the principles of dharma, but inasmuch as the principles of dharma are unknown and as whatever that is good is regarded as dharma, the question whether caste-system is *dharma* or *adharma* means only whether caste-system is good or bad.

Scientific inquiry in this volume.—This volume has two-fold aspects. The first is historical. This aspect consists in narrating the development of a particular society, and to this narration a forecast regarding the future and a polity to determine the future have been added. The other aspect is scientific and philosophical. A theory of social evolution is described with the help of facts which come within the scope. Exploitation of this philosophical aspect made it necessary to make the following digressions in logic.

(i) Definition of a religion, and the principles of the scientific study of religions.

(ii) Ethnological classification and its place in the history of man.

Scientific study of religion and theology.—The use of the term *religion* in general social science is condemned, though the word theology is admitted as a scientific term. No attempt is made to give a system of scientific principles for the study of theology. Still inasmuch as the theological ideas of people have had serious influence on the lives of individuals and societies, the previous scientific effort of the Hindus on this subject is presented in the second chapter under the title Hindu Terminology so far as it touches the subject.

This terminology has not been a result of a narrow system. It is a terminology suitable for the scientific treatment of those social phenomena which have been created by the theological ideas, and which pervade the whole world. I have given that terminology in detail because I think that it is to be of permanent value to science. This analysis will also show how the theological ideas and social questions are rigorously kept apart in the Hindu thought. It is also shown that the only case in which these two separate departments of ideas are mixed is in the case of the religions that are in the traditions of theophratry (sampradāya).

Explanation of Hinduism.—As Hinduism, that is, the Hindu community or its traditions, has not been formed by the process of theophratry the process which led to the formation of Hinduism has been discussed in the third chapter. Here I have shown that the different tribes and castes under Hinduism, though of heterogeneous origin, acquired conception of unity, and that this body, though non-theological, distinguished itself from foreign theophratries (sampradāyas) like Christianity and Mohamedanism which follow unsacred conduct. I then proceeded to describe the internal ties which bind the various castes and tribes under Hinduism, and showed how the Hindus developed a cosmopolitan philosophy (chap. IV) as they have produced a cosmopolitan terminology. In the case of theophratry the admission to or expulsion from the body is easy, similarity of belief gives admission and dissimilarity causes a fall. But in the case of Hinduism, which is not a theophratry, admission to Hindu society or expulsion from Hinduism is rendered difficult (chap. V). To explain as to how the modern conditions have affected the matter of expulsion from the Hindu society, and also how the Hindu society itself is changing its traditions rapidly and making the entire Hindu society better fit for the future world-community, I have described modern social conditions (chap. VI).

One question which troubles the minds of thinkers when they examine Hinduism is what is orthodoxy, and what is heterodoxy under Hinduism; that question is explained in the seventh chapter. The next three chapters expound the theoretical portion of the evolution of Hinduism and other developments, and make a forecast regarding the future of existing institutions, and discuss the question of reforming Hinduism in the light of the forecast.

The theory of Evolution in the book.—The book, while explaining the formation of Hindu society and making a forecast regarding the future development of Hinduism into Indianism, expounds a theory of evolution from facts which come within the history of Hinduism. This theory of evolution is scattered in three or four places. Starting from a point when the world was full of roving tribes each having to do very little with the others and when large political bodies and social philosophy or theology to bind numbers of tribes into larger groups were non-existent, I have tried to summarize the processes which have made the world of to-day as it is. The provisional theory preceding this point and the scientific method for restoring the history of tribes, have been discussed in the Appendix II. The main portion of this book is given to throw light on some phases of social evolution resulting from the communications and commerce of the tribes. In the chapter VIII on the theory of social evolution, I have described two types of tribes, viz. *natural tribes* and *theophratries* and the two processes of the formation of the larger bodies, namely, the *process of contact* and the *process of religions* or *theophratries*. Of the causes which bring about larger social groups and larger social consciousness, I have described two, namely the spread of religions and political conquest. I have then described the process called by the term *integration* which welds the communities brought together under one system into one social group.

I have shown that the process of integration of society had not been working in India as there was no successful attempt made by any Hindu state to bring India under one control, and also because no theophratry had succeeded in absorbing the whole of India. In the next chapter on the future of Hinduism I have described two factors which will create integration of Indian society—namely: (i) insistence on the ideal of territorial community as against the tribal conception, and (ii) the creation of national aristocracy. This territorial ideal could be achieved (*a*) by the creation of common territorial tradition, and territorial law; (*b*) by increase in the assimilative powers of the community.

The chapters on the future of Hinduism and future of religions involve speculation regarding the future of India and also of the entire world. The forecast is made to the effect that the civilization of the world will be unified. It is shown that the present conditions of India and of Hinduism are such that they may find a fit place in the future cosmopolitanism. Both India and the Western world are preparing themselves unconsciously for the same goal. Secularization of politics in its purest form means not to allow theological ideas to be the determinant of the social group. Staunch and rigorous observance of this principle is necessary for the unity of civilization. How the Western world is approaching this ideal is just described. In India politics under Hinduism were strictly secular. It is only under the subjection of foreign theophratries that connexion between politics and religion is brought into existence.

Future of Tribal Culture.—The fates of theophratries and also of the federated tribal society of Hinduism is discussed. I may here make some remarks regarding the fates of the tribes unconnected with Hinduism.

The future of the natural tribe is to be absorbed in a larger tribe or help to form a culture common to many tribes. This type of tribe does very little of adoption of individual outsiders. But the theophratries try to take in members from other communities by a process called conversion.

The following are the factors in which the two different types of tribes resemble. These factors again produce a feeling of unity.

(i) Common head. (ii) Common worship. (iii) Common festival. (iv) Common history and tradition.

Sometimes the natural tribe loses political independence but still keeps its tribal individuality. This happens to be the case when the tribe has a strong literary tradition.

In such a case the features of the tribe which remain are worship, customs and philosophy. The political interest of the tribe is looked after by another tribe and the former has to follow laws made by the latter. The worship and the traditional sacred books are the only heritage of the tribe and these keep the tribe in touch with the past and separate from the other people around them. Very often if such a tribe is surrounded by a dominant theophratry, which may be stealing members from the tribe, then the tribe becomes extremely anxious to keep its own culture and tradition and tries to make itself a theophratry, so that people could come in their tribe by accepting similar worship. But should such a tribe unconnected with religion remain dominant in a country where the theophratries are present then the traditions and ritual of the tribe becomes the State ceremonial as it is in the case of the Japanese.

History of Caste is not History of four Varṇas.— The history of caste in India comprises two distinct studies. On one hand it becomes simply a study of social theories and of their developments. For example, the history of four Varṇas (chāturvarṇya) is not a history of changes in the society to a very great extent. The theory of four varṇas had been of very little influence in making and unmaking social groups. Nevertheless inasmuch as ideas influence social conditions and events and are influenced by them, the doctrine of four varṇas received a considerable development when the people who held it came in contact with new peoples and conditions. As they held this doctrine strongly, the doctrine created feelings of respect, fear, and contempt towards certain peoples and communities. But this theory, as I have said, did not do much to make and unmake social groups.

The four varṇas in India were never four castes. The history of caste in India is not a history of the multiplication of castes out of the original four. The belief that all the three thousand castes have been the result of the splitting of the original four castes is hopelessly wrong. The theory of four varṇas originally implied that every society is divided into four classes and that these classes are made according to their function (karma) in society and according to their merit.

When the Brāhmaṇas held fast the theory of four varṇas and thought that the varṇa was something similar to a jati (as they themselves were both varṇa and jati) they began to imagine that the various castes in India which have different caste names are either products of the mixture of the original four castes or due to the degradation of a section of the four castes. Some of the castes and tribes were classed by them as Kshatriyas, some as Vaishyas, and some as Shūdras. This classification was not made by them in any systematic manner taking all the castes and tribes in India into consideration. Their classification was casual. Every case was decided as it came. They followed one rule. Every tribe or person they may come in contact with was a Shūdra unless there is some special reason to class any of these as Vaishya or Kshatriya. Thus the history of four varṇas means the history of classifications of the various tribes and definitions of each of the four varṇas in terms of castes. It also includes the further development of the four varṇa theory.

History of the Development of Hindu Community.—The facts regarding the history of the Hindu community may thus be summarized.

Prior to the immigration of the Rigvedic Aryans India

was full of many tribes, many of which probably exist even to-day. These tribes belonged to different races, and it is also possible that there were many Āryan tribes in India prior to Rigvedic immigration. All these different tribes had probably no other superior than tribal consciousness.

With the immigration of the Aryans, a new culture came to India. That culture received good development in the upper valley of the Ganges. Development of this culture and the rise of the Brahmaṇas, first as a class and then as a caste, were probably contemporaneous. These Brahmaṇas migrated all over India. They migrated as a caste, and the various castes of the Brahmaṇas have been caused by the process of subdivision mostly. Some writers claim that some Brahmaṇas were made out of tribal priests, but the evidence offered for the statement has been too scanty to express an opinion either one way or the other. As these Brahmaṇas travelled they carried with them the idea of four varṇas, and tried to apply that idea to local conditions. The king of the place and perhaps his near relatives became Kshatriyas. Some people they called vaishyas and some others they called shudras. The conditions of different localities varied and so the possibilities of making out four classes in that locality also were varied.

The people who belonged to Kshatriya varṇa probably did not meet each other. There was no Kshatriya consciousness excepting in small parts. Again, whether a particular tribe or family was Kshatriya or not was always indefinite. The ruler of the part could easily become a Kshatriya, but how many people in the tribe besides the ruler were to be recognized as Kshatriya was a matter of great difficulty. In many places only the ruler was recognized as Kshatriya on account of his office, and when the ruling family disappeared Kshatriyas also disappeared. Brāhmana varṇa was composed of those who were descended from the same stock. They migrated and thus became different castes. This varṇa did not contain many intruders, and so their body was definite and had a communal consciousness. But this was not the case with the Kshatriyas. The Kshatriyas were tribes and families of heterogeneous origin of various races entirely unknown to each other. Those families or tribes whom the Brahmaṇas made into Kshatriyas knew that they were Kshatriyas but did not know who else did.

The Kshatriya consciousness never developed a communal feeling because the class of Kshatriyas in each locality did not know the Kshatriyas in other localities. A family, for example, in a certain caste (jāti) would be regarded as a Kshatriya while the rest of the people would be considered as Shudras. The constitution of Kshatriya varṇa differed from that of the Brāhmaṇa varṇa in two respects, Kshatriyas were not a federation of castes. They were not again of the same origin. They did not have even a tradition of the same origin, excepting the allegorical and mystic verse from Purushsukta.

When the Brahmaṇas migrated in different parts of India and abroad, they helped to create a unity of civilization. The process by which this unity of civilization was created is described in the further pages.

Caste System and Hindu Theology and Social Philosophy. —To the question as to what relation the caste system bears to Hindu religion a reply may be given as follows:

There is no "Hindu religion." "Hinduism," which means the Hindu society and its tradition, is not a religion, but is akin to tribal or national culture. Hindu society was not created on any principles previously laid down.

Hinduism has theology and social philosophy of great antiquity continued to the present day. The theology which Hindus, especially the Brahmaṇas, created belonged to various schools. Some schools of theology were silent about castes and the theories of the most orthodox school (Vedantic) discountenance caste system in the most uncompromising manner.

The most dominant social doctrine which has shaped the Hindu thought for nearly two thousand years, is the doctrine of four varṇas, which recognizes and even insists on the fact that every society should consist of various classes and occupations, and the distribution of the various positions in life on the basis of merit and accomplishment (karma). The doctrine of four varṇas, if properly understood, is a very healthy doctrine for any people. This doctrine does not support the caste system but is antagonistic to it. When the Brahmaṇas insisted on this doctrine, in most cases their attempts were not blameworthy. Still it is necessary to change that doctrine now. Much error has been caused in the interpretation of the Brāhmaṇic social ideals, and specially in the interpretation of this Brāhmaṇical doctrine. This error is due to the fact that the study of Hindu social philosophy, which deserves great attention, has been neglected.

Not only the theology and the varṇa doctrine have been opposed to the Hindu caste system but so has been their "dharma" philosophy. What dharma writers insist on is that everybody should perform the duties of his position (varṇa). This dharma doctrine of the Hindus does not endorse caste system.

These statements made regarding theology and social

philosophy have been results of research, but I do not propose to present that research in this volume.

Reception of the first Volume.—Passing remarks regarding the reception of the first volume by the public may be made here. The volume did not have a very good sale. Still, as far as reviews are concerned, most of the reviews have been very flattering to the author.

Two men of world-wide reputation for Sanskrit and Pali scholarship have done honour to the author by reviewing his book. This book again attracted considerable attention among the sociologists in America and Continental Europe, and some well-known sociologists wrote reviews. Even the late Sir H. Risley generously wrote to me complimenting on the book and admitting the justice of my criticism of his speculations and to say that his speculations were intended only to stimulate discussion and research on the subject. Somehow or other the book attracted considerable attention in America, much less in England and almost no attention in India. As far as I could locate the sales in India less than twenty copies have been sold in India within two years, apart from the order for fifty copies given by the education department of the state of Baroda. This statement may be humiliating to the author, but I make it in order to illustrate how my countrymen appreciate a scientific work on caste, even though they have a great deal of enthusiasm to talk against the caste system.

Acknowledgements.—I take opportunity here to thank His Highness Shri Sayajirao Gaikwar, the Maharaja of Baroda, whose generous aid for three years permitted me to pursue my studies in America, and to continue my labours in the History of Caste.

In connexion with the second volume, it is necessary to make mention of the courtesy of Dr. L. D. Barnett of the British Museum, who went over the manuscript and made some valuable suggestions.

CONTENTS

CHAPTER I

PAGE

DEFINITION OF A "RELIGION"

CHAPTER II

HINDU TERMINOLOGY

CHAPTER III

Hindu Social Theory

PAGE

CHAPTER IV

Internal Ties

PAGE

CHAPTER V

Membership of Hinduism

CHAPTER VI

Modern Social Conditions

CHAPTER VII

Orthodoxy and Heterodoxy

CHAPTER VIII

Theory of Social Evolution

CHAPTER IX

Future of Hinduism

CHAPTER X

APPENDIX I

APPENDIX II

CHAPTER I

DEFINITION OF A "RELIGION"

THE words, Hinduism, Hindu religion, Brahmanism, etc., are of European coinage. In Sanskrit there is no word which can convey the exact meaning or the exact number of meanings which the word "religion" conveys to the Western world. At present, the word "religion" is translated in the modern Indian languages like Marathi and Hindi by the word "dharma"; but the latter word, taken as it is from Sanskrit, with a traditional meaning of its own, conveys to a Hindu mind a set of ideas entirely different from those which are conveyed to Christians by the word "religion." "Religion" is, in fact, a word extremely abused, and it is of questionable value as a term in the comparative study of civilizations, or in a general social science; though it may be useful in the study of European civilization. What I propose to do here is to state the different conceptions that are involved in the word "religion" in the popular mind, so far as I can understand them. I shall then discuss whether the term "religion" can be applied to Hinduism.

When a Christian thinks of religion he generally conceives of a system characterized by the following ideas.

He first of all thinks, that a religion should explain questions like, what is God? what becomes of man after his death ? and so forth. That is, it should give information regarding the unseen and unknown.

He again thinks that religion should contain admonitions regarding conduct. If the religion be personal, that is, brought into existence by Individuals like Jesus, Mohamed, Buddha, the teachings of that Son of God, or prophet or philosopher should become the guiding principles of life for its followers. He also expects that the moral injunctions of a religion should be definite.

He also thinks that a religion should have an authoritative scripture, like the Bible or the Koran. Such scriptures are, in fact, essential in order to make the moral injunctions of the religion definite.

He also thinks of certain ceremonies, rituals and sacraments as part of the religion, and holds that adhesion to those things is compulsory on the followers of religion. In the Christian Church (for example) baptism, marriage by a Christian minister, etc., are considered compulsory.

He also thinks that a religion is not only an adviser in morals, etc., but is supreme in the field. In deciding whether a certain action is good or not, the authority of religion should receive supreme consideration, and should even be regarded as final. He also thinks that the laws and customs of the country which professes a certain religion should conform to and must not oppose scriptural injunctions.

Another thing which he expects of a religion is that it should be a system, the injunctions of which should create very strong sentiments among its followers. Thus, when he says that a particular belief or attitude is his religion, he means that that attitude is his strongest sentiment. He expects a devout Christian to be so imbued with the teachings of Christ that his reflex actions should accord with those teachings.

One more thing which he expects of a religion is that the religion should become formative or determinative of the social group. He believes that those who follow the same religion belong, or should belong, to the same society; and those who forsake that religion should be considered as outside that society. This notion is being gradually forsaken to-day, and at present specially in America there seems to be an attempt to make other things than religion the prime determinant of the social group. Political allegiance, and race, appear to tend more and more to displace the religious considerations, in the determination of a social group.

Religious excommunication to-day does not mean a social exclusion. Still even to-day religion is a factor not to be ignored. When people wish to make a reference to that social group consisting of peoples in Europe and America, they call that group Christendom, and this group is connected by a strong bond of sympathy because of Christianity. The word "heathen" is still full of meaning to the American people. This word conveys to their minds a notion of unspeakable savages or semi-civilized people. Still it does not connote to them the negro in that country. A Chinaman appears before their vision when that word is uttered.

All this religious system with its ethical ideals, its sacraments, and sentimental fervour and devotion towards its institutor and his teachings, is considered as a preparatory requirement to attain heaven or some kind of eternal bliss, for creatures possessed with souls, which according to the Christian belief are human beings only.

If we wish to include all these ideas in a formal definition, we may define religion as it is understood by the occidental people generally in the following manner.

Religion is a system with two characteristics :—

First, it is intended to attain some kind of eternal bliss defined by its own ideas regarding God and future life and obtainable by adhesion to certain definite ceremonies and sacraments and by adhesion to the teachings regarding conduct and morals of some definite teacher or school of teachers conveyed by means of some authoritative scripture modelling the sentiments of the followers strongly; and to which all the laws and customs of the country professing allegiance to it ought to conform.

And secondly, it makes all its followers one strong social group by a community of feelings and interests.

I should like to inform the readers that this definition when I formed it was intended to be purely objective. The definition did not give my idea of the thing, but my idea of the idea. I was not seeking to explain what "religion" is, but only what "religion" is understood to be by the Western world. My attitude herein was not that of a modern theologian who might wish to explain what God is, but that of a historian desirous of explaining what ideas the ancients had regarding the gods Jupiter or Yahweh.

After framing this definition I realized that it could be made of some value to social science.

When I say that this definition could be useful in social sciences, it should not be supposed that I am going to adopt this as a scientific term for general social science. Such a term would be useful in studying the European civilization, just as the term "Obeah" could be of use in interpreting the civilization of the West Indian negroes.

The word "religion" has acquired a complex meaning, as given above; at the same time in non-European languages there is not a word which can convey the same number of correlated ideas. Such a condition of affairs is not merely an accident. It is due to the fact that the course of events in Europe has been different from the course of events in India. Those different courses of events have created a vocabulary expressive of ideas peculiar to the civilization itself. Thus the word religion would be of use to delineate the development of occidental civilization and ideas. To undertake the task of explaining this development would be out of place here; still one phase of it may be noted.

Let us state the preceding analysis and synthesis of religion in a different manner. We may first class systems like Christianity among the *theophratries*, that is, among the brotherhoods based on worships or on some theological doctrines. Thus religions would be akin to what pantha or sampradāya is in India. But "religion" is something more than a theophratry (sampradāya). "Sampradāya" is not quite so strong a word in India as "religion" is in Europe. No sampradāya played such an important part in shaping the moral and intellectual history of India as the sampradāya (of Christ) did in Europe. The theophratry of Christ and its traditions gave to Europe a code of morals, theology, laws, superstitions and a great number of ideas regarding production of the world, and so forth. No theophratry in India accomplished such a task. As a result of this, "sampradāya" does not convey so many ideas as religion does and has not become so strong a word, meaning everything essential for life, as religion has become. For the same reason the Hindu mind (until it was vitiated by European conceptions) was spared the confusion which causes troubles to European minds when they wish to distinguish between " religion " and morality, or religion and philosophy, or between other similar absurd comparisons.

Comparing Christianity with Judaism we find one essential difference : Christianity is the tradition of a theophratry and Judaism is a tradition of a natural tribe.

CHAPTER II

HINDU TERMINOLOGY

I HAVE advocated that the phenomena should be first analysed so as to separate the like from the unlike. It is impracticable to enter here into a complete analysis of a civilization into its most elementary or ultimate factors. We should confine our attention here to only such factors as may help us to study "religions" and express their relation to the social organization. Something has already been done by the Hindus in this direction, and their analysis deserves to be stated here, as in the first place it should help us to understand the Hindu civilization, and secondly, part of their classification should be of value to a general social science and to a scientific study of religions. The various factors which are put together in the occidental conception of religion have been distinguished and their mutual relationship has already been established. There is no word in Sanskrit which now causes so much trouble as the word "religion" does in English. The various concepts above referred to are—

(1) Dharma, or Duty.

(2) Mārga (sādhana), Path by which the desired good result (sādhya) like heaven, absorption into Brahma, nirvāna or Godhood or Buddhahood can be attained.

(3) " Mata " means the doctrine, specially regarding the nature of God.

(4) Sampradāya means the following of a teacher or of a school of teachers, the membership of which enables a man to seek God or the other desired bliss.

(5) Sādhya is the object to be attained, like heaven, absorption in the Brahma, etc.

The terms given above are but a small portion of the large number of terms which exist in the science. The various ideas of the Hindus in this subject have been reduced to one single system, but a unity terminology has not yet been attained. I shall try to present the ideas held and the terms used by the orthodox writers with as much consistency as possible.

I have already stated that the word " religion " is translated by Hindus by the word " dharma," and also that it is a bad translation, as the ideas conveyed to the mind of a Hindu by the word " dharma " are yet different from those conveyed to the European mind by the word " religion." In order to convey a correct idea of the Hindu theological and moral system it would be better for me to give first of all the Hindu theory of dharma. It is as follows :—

To all things animate or inanimate, dharma (qualities) has been assigned at the original creation. For example, the dharma of gold is yellow colour and brightness ; the dharma of stone is weight, etc. ; the dharma of tiger is ferocity and eating other animals ; the dharma of a deer is nimbleness. When they speak of Mānava-dharma, they mean both " dharma of man " and " dharma for man " ; that is, they either mean human characteristics or qualities, or qualities and conduct proper for man, which are, in their turn, determined by the human qualities. All the rules of morality which every man is expected to follow are called dharma for man (Mānava-dharma).

But that dharma for man is only a small part of dharma which a particular individual has to follow. Dharma for an individual is dependent on his civil condition and position in life. The dharma for a king is different from the dharma for a subject. Dharma for a householder is different from the dharma for a single man, and so forth.

Man is again a member of a family, of a tribe, of a caste, and of a corporation (Gaṇa). He has then to follow the dharma peculiar to that family, caste, or corporation.

Dharma for a man is different from the dharma for a woman. Dharma for a woman also differs according to her status, like maidenhood, wifehood or widowhood.

Thus a particular individual is bound by his duties or dharmas of various kinds. He has to follow first of all Mānava-dharma, that is, his duties as a man or as a member of humanity. On this subject the precept of Manu is this. Abstention from injuring creatures, veracity, abstention from unlawfully appropriating the goods of others, purity and control of organs, Manu has declared to be the summary of dharma for the four (all) classes.[1] In addition to man's duties as a man, he has to follow also the dharma of his class (Varṇa). Moreover, he has to attend to his obligations as a householder, as a husband, as a father of a family, as a son, and so forth. He should also pay attention to the dharma particular to his family, and to his jāti or caste.

The nature of different dharmas can be easily understood. What a man should do in order to fulfil his obliga-

[1] Manu x. 63.

tions, as a member of humanity, or as a husband or father, would involve more or less the same duties as a Westerner would imagine them to be. Perhaps the jāti-dharma and Kula-dharma need some explanation.

Jāti-dharma, or the duties of a man as a member of a tribe, generally consists of obeying the laws of the tribe regarding marriage and divorce, etc., the worship of tribal gods and general participation in the rites and festivals of the tribe. Kula-dharma is something similar. Here an individual is expected to follow the customs of the family.

How should a person know his dharma? How should he know what his duties are towards humanity, towards his class, tribe, and for his civil condition? The general advice on the matter is that he should guide his conduct by the practice of the best of his class. "Vedas are the first source of dharma, next come smṛitis, and then the virtuous conduct of those who know the Vedas and the customs of holy-men, and finally self-satisfaction." [1] Every man generally follows the customs of his tribe and is governed by ideas of right or wrong that prevail in the tribe. The tribe follows its own tradition, and in cases of doubt as to what is proper they consult the Brāhmaṇas.

No pretence is made to the effect that everything regarding dharma is known, for it is infinite and eternal. The orthodox belief is that whenever dharma becomes faded the God proclaims it through inspired persons. There is no restriction as to who should give advice on dharma. Any learned man, that is, learned according to Hindu standards, who is speaker of truth may explain dharma. Even though dharma is regarded as infinite and unknowable in totality, it is not regarded as a great grievance, for every

[1] Manu ii. 6.

man is expected to follow dharma as much as he knows it. What a man is expected to do is to follow the example of winged creatures, who do not know where the firmament ends, but penetrate it as far as they can.

Hindus have no word for their traditions in Sanskrit. Hinduism, Brahmanism, Vedism are words of European coinage. The reason why they do not have any special word is that for a long time they were unconscious of their speciality. Later on, when they became conscious of the fact, then new words began to be coined. Hindus follow "dharma," which is only one and eternal, and which, according to Hindu belief, is something which all men follow in proportion to their intellect. When the dharma was in the process of development Hindus, or rather the Brāhmaṇas, had no idea as to whether there are any other people in the world who may reject their system of dharma.

The word Christianity is translated in modern Indian languages like Marathi, by words like "Khristi-dharma" or "Khrista-mārga." But these words do not convey the same idea to them as the word Christianity does to the Western people. A Hindu looks up "Khristi-dharma" as a tribal dharma, that is, the duties of following the customs and the ceremonies and the worship of a tribal God, i.e. Christ, and some other duties, which a member of the Christian tribe may follow. That is, they do not look upon Christianity the sole or even adequate guide to conduct even for the people who belong to the tribe called Christians. The Christians have to follow Mānava-dharma, that is their duties as the members of humanity. They also have to follow the dharma for a man as a member of the family; and so forth. In addition to these duties Christians follow customs of their own tribe, like communion and baptism. When they use the word "Khrista-mārga," ("path of Christ") they mean the path which Christ advised His disciples to follow in order to secure eternal bliss. They look upon "Christianity" in the same way as they look upon different sampradāyas under Hinduism, like Jainism, Mahānubhāva and others. The word "mārga" means "the way." These mārgas are divided on various principles.

They are called after the teacher or expounder, or after the doctrine. The latter nomenclature only is adopted by intelligent men. According to the doctrine there is a threefold division of the mārgas, i.e., knowledge, devotion, and action. The orthodox school or the Vedanta school thinks that the eternal bliss can be reached by knowledge only. The Bhāgavata school laid stress on Bhakti or devotion, but they consider devotion as merely a preparation to accept the path of knowledge. They would say that the theories of Vedanta are too difficult for ignorant people, and before they could attain the stage, proper for the acceptance of knowledge as a path to eternal bliss they would go astray. Even Tukārāma, the great advocate of devotion, has said: The end (the knowledge and attainment of Brahma) is all that it is necessary to attain, and all the troubles (of worship and prayer) are only prior to it; those who know the path directly are rare among men. The Karma-mārga, which consists of following the Vedic practices, held nearly the same attitude. The path of knowledge is considered the supreme one, a path beyond the reach of ignorant persons.

Hindu theologians who have studied Christianity have found that the Khrista-mārga is nothing but the mārga of devotion. They thus expect that those Christians who should reach a higher stage of intellect would take up the path of knowledge instead of the path of devotion, and of fervent prayer to the deity.

When Hindus or specially Brāhmaṇas try to understand the Christian religion, they naturally begin to analyse and examine Christianity in accordance with their habitual mode of thought. They first try to ascertain the dharma of Christians. They hold that an eternal and infinite thing like dharma cannot be divided after the expounder, but it may be divided according to status, tribe or family. To divide the dharma knowledge by the expounder instead of by the subject matter is regarded as an irrational and illogical method of division. If there be any moral ideas in Christianity, they class them with the moral ideas that are common in all creeds and people, and thus recognize that even the tribe of Christians have some ideas of Mānava-dharma, that is, duties of man as a member of humanity. The ideas and customs which they find peculiar to Christians are the customs of eating beef and drinking liquor, and worshipping the tribal gods, the Father, the Son, and the Holy Ghost and Mary, and a host of saints, and the observance of Christmas, Easter and Good Friday. This is considered by them the peculiar dharma of the Christian tribe. The propaganda of Christianity to them means, propaganda of these customs and not the propaganda of the duties of man as a member of humanity, for the latter to them cannot be anything else than their own Mānava-dharma. Mānava-dharma (Dharma of Humanity) is only one and eternal, and thus there cannot be two conflicting orders of Mānava-dharma.

The religions or sects based upon the teachings of particular men are sometimes called "mata." This word means thought, doctrine or opinions, Buddhism is very often called "Bauddha-mata," the "opinion" of the Buddhists. These "matas" generally represent the fundamental principles of doctrines of the system. The word "Khrista-mata" is also occasionally used in Marathi literature. This is done by men who wish to deny the possibility of Christianity being classed as any definite dharma or mārga. Among the Christian doctrines (mata) they include beliefs like the following :— (i) All men and possibly women are possessed of an object called "soul," while no other creatures have any soul; (ii) Salvation can be attained through faith in Christ; (iii) There is a personal god; (iv) The world created and ruled by two distinct individuals, God and the Devil; (v) Sin is the creation of the Devil. Some Hindu students of Christianity would also include in the matas the Christian conceptions of Heaven and Hell.

Thus, some fundamental differences in the ideas of Western people and the ideas of the Hindus are reflected, in the fact that Hindus find it necessary to translate the word "religion" with three different words: Dharma, Mārga, and Mata. There is no word in Sanskrit expressive of a system containing all these three entities. Those differences are mainly these. Dharma, or duties of man as a member of mankind, state, or clan, has so very little relation to the ideas which men may have regarding the nature of God, soul, etc., that to put all these together into a coherent system would not be justifiable. Western people generally imagine their interdependence simply because both of them emanate from the same source, the Bible, and for another reason which will be explained later. According to Hindu theory, even a person who may feel doubtful regarding the existence of God or the life after death is still and must be a follower of dharma. Though the theologians believed that a life led according to the principles of dharma will lead to the eternal bliss, they regarded it only as a probable result. Dharma according to the advisers on the question is to be followed for its own sake, and irrespective of any reward. They also advised that as men need some motive for action, the adhesion to dharma should be done with the belief that the adhesion will do good some time.

Dharma is distinct from "the path" advised by a person, inasmuch as the path came into existence at a definite period, while dharma is eternal. The "path" (mārga) and the "doctrine" (mata), combined together, are often expressed by one word, "sampradāya," which literally means "that which is given," that is, an established doctrine transmitted from a teacher to disciples. This "sampradāya" nearly corresponds with the Western conception of a "religion."

Dharma itself is a great field of knowledge. It is subdivided in various ways. No systematic treatment of all subdivisions has yet been made. The various ways in which the various subdivisions are made by Sanskrit and Prakrit writers are as follows:—

First method divides dharma into (1) dharma for individual (Purusha-dharma, or Vyakti-dharma), (2) dharma respecting family (Kula-dharma), and (3) dharma respecting the tribe or caste (Jāti-dharma), and (4) dharma respecting the nation or the country (Desha-dharma, or Rāshtra-dharma).

When these various dharmas conflict with each other, that is, when the duties towards one group conflict with the duties towards another, the only rule laid down, both by dharma writers and writers on niti (conduct) is that the interests of the smaller group should be sacrificed to the larger. On this matter the guiding verse tells us " For the sake of the family (kula) individual (purusha) should be abandoned, for the sake of town (Grāma) even the family should be abandoned, and for the sake of the country the town may be abandoned." Another method divides dharma into, dharma regarding personal ceremonial conduct (āchāra); ordinary court law (Vyavahāra-dharma) rules regarding penance (Prāyaschitta-dharma). Dharma is also divided according to sex (Linga-dharma) into dharma for man (Purusha-dharma) and dharma for woman (Strī-dharma).

Dharma for the individual differs according to the class (varna) to which he belongs; according to this division there are four divisions of dharma, namely, Brāhmaṇa-dharma, Kshatriya-dharma, Vaishya-dharma, and Shūdra-dharma. To these some writers add Antyaja-dharma, viz. dharma for the outcasts.

Dharma is also classified according to the Āshrama of the individual. These āshramas are four as far as Ārya men are concerned. They are, (1) Student (Brāhma-charya), (2), Householder (Grihastha), (3) Forest-dweller (Vānaprastha), and (4) Ascetic (Sanyasta).

Though there are several ways in which dharma is divided, the dharma is by no means completely exhausted. There is always some room for innovation and addition. For example, in the seventeenth century, a new word was coined and a new dharma was created, by the famous Maratha sage Rāmadāsa. He called it Maharāshtra-dharma, a word which is used by the writers in Mahārāshtra (the Maratha country), in two senses. It means first of all the duties of the Marathas, and secondly it means the duties of a great nation (i.e. the Marathas).

New writings are always rising and the dharma is still capable of further exploitation.

The words "Hindu dharma" are being used to-day. But the import of the words is not settled. It is in a state of confusion, which is by the way due to the fact that the English conception of the word "religion" is trying to displace the old meaning of the word "dharma" in order to appropriate that word for itself. It is not likely that the conception of religion will be ever poured into the word dharma successfully. All that it has achieved to-day is that it has created temporary confusion in ideas, which is bound to disappear before the march of science and scholarship. According to the orthodox usage, the words "Hindu dharma" and "Ārya dharma" are synonymous. The words "Hindu dharma" were used in the vulgar or ordinary conversation, while the words "Ārya dharma" were used in a dignified conversation. In the orthodox usage the word *dharma* kept its original meaning. Ārya-dharma simply means the conduct and usage that are proper for a gentleman (Ārya). The word ārya-dharma refers neither to any gods of the Hindu pantheon nor to any of the philosophical tenets. It refers primarily to the question of conduct. "Ārya-dharma" is contrasted with the dharma of non-Hindu communities, like Christian or Mohamedan, by the term "Mlechchha-dharma," the dharma of the barbarian. They contrasted the dharmas thus by observing the facts regarding the conduct of themselves and those of Christian and Mohamedan. As the conduct of the Christians did not favourably impress them, they called their conduct "Mlechchha-dharma."

Thus the great difference between the Hindu conception of the "dharma" and the European conception of "religion" is this. To a European, Christianity or Christian religion are self-defined terms, and the acceptance of those ideas and practices that are indicated by the word would make a man Christian. In the case of Hindu-dharma, the relation is different. Hindus are a definite body, and "Hindu-dharma" is that indefinite thing which the Hindus consider their own dharma.

I have said that the word "sampradāya" comes very near the word "religion." If this is the case, a question may be asked: why do the Hindus regard a religion like Christianity merely as a tribal tradition?

The reason is this: many sampradāyas give rise to castes and tribes. The teacher and his disciples tend to form an exclusive community. If they do so they simply become tribes, open to those who wish to come in. The tribes which sampradāyas or religions give rise to are trying to extend their membership, but for that reason they do not cease to be exclusive, as they restrict the social intercourse of the members to the people who are already in the tribe. There are some sampradāyas in India that do not disturb the existing social arrangement by the foundation of new tribes, and therefore such sampradāyas are regarded as orthodox and are generally tolerated. But those sampradāyas which make theological doctrine, cult or a mode of worship a pretence to form a new tribe are hated as heterodox, and in my opinion the antipathy shown to them is perfectly reasonable. When Europeans see that Hindus hate the spread of Christianity and the rise and spread of other missionary religions, they interpret it as a dislike on the part of a caste-loving Hindu against a religion of equality. But this interpretation is incorrect. The Hindu antipathy is due to the fact that these religions, or sampradāyas, merely add to the already existing castes, and by their missionary zeal try to foster one caste at the expense of the rest.

CHAPTER III

HINDU SOCIAL THEORY

IT is necessary to present here some phases of the Hindu social theory. I have already said that the Hindu society is a system of castes. According to Hindu theory the whole world is divided into a number of jātis, i.e., castes or tribes. These jātis differ from each other as far as sacredness and purity are concerned. While Brāhmaṇas, who are always pure in speech and action, who increase their personal sacredness by the study of the Vedas and eating only pure food, are holiest and therefore at the top, the tribes like Christians and Mohamedans, who are characterized by cruelty and by the use of impure food, are most impure.[1]

[1] I should also state here that Christians and Mohamedans are regarded as impure, but not on account of their belief in their respective Saviour and prophets and their teaching. What belief a man follows is not a matter of serious importance to a Hindu. The question to which they attach great importance is whether the particular tribe and the individuals therein do any actions (karma) that are impure. If they do those actions, then those tribes are impure. Had Christians abstained from killing cows, and drinking liquor, the Hindus would not have regarded them as impure people. This may be illustrated from the attitude of the Brāhmanas towards the Jains. The Jains' belief is different from that of the Brāhmaṇas and their followers. They deny the authority of the Brāhmaṇas, still even the orthodox Brāhmaṇas in the Maratha country, especially in Berar, do not seem to have any objection to

Theoretically, the distance between a Brāhmaṇa and a Paria is not different in kind from the distance between a Brāhmaṇa and a Kāyastha. Similarly the distance between a Brāhmaṇa and a caste like that of carpenters or goldsmiths is not different in kind from the distance between a Brāhmaṇa and a Christian or Mohamedan. All these are separated from each other only in a degree, and not in kind. The cause which keeps the different groups distant is the amount of purity or pollution which is supposed to be attached to each of the groups. According to Hindu notions, then, the whole world is a single community grouped in a hierarchy with the Brāhmaṇas at the head.

Why then should there be any line between Hindus on one hand and Christians and Mohamedans on the other? The fact is that this line has not been drawn by the Hindus, but by the followers of Mohamedanism, Christianity, Zorastrianism, and Judaism. Religious opinion was not and is not a matter which would separate a man from his social group, or would admit a foreigner to any social group. Only when a number of persons who believe similarly form a sect with a separate social existence, and when that sect would make a convert a member socially, then only would a man who should join that sect be separated from his own social group; that is, he would go out of his own caste, and would join that caste which would open its doors to him. Thus when a man becomes a Christian

drink water from their hands, though these Brāhmaṇas show an objection to drink water touched by such high castes as Kunbimaratha, Goldsmith, Kayastha Prabhu, and even Sārasvata Brāhmaṇa. The reason for this attitude is merely this: the Jains, like the Brāhmaṇas of Mahārāshtra, abstain from the use of animal food, while the other high castes named above do not abstain from it.

according to the Hindu standpoint, he leaves his own caste and joins that of the Christians.

What is then the distinction between a Hindu and a non-Hindu. To answer this question, one must pay attention to history. The word *Hindu* itself is a foreign one. The Hindus never used it in any Sanskrit writing, that is those which were written before the Mohamedan invasion. In fact there was no need for calling themselves by any particular name. People in India were as a rule ignorant, or at least indifferent towards the existence of other countries and peoples in the world. They became acquainted with foreigners only when those foreigners visited the country, either in the capacity of merchants, travellers or invaders. But such a foreigner always belonged to a certain tribe, and passed among Hindus as a member of that tribe. In the early days when the foreigners came, the difference between the people of India and the foreigners was not very great. Those foreigners would take up Hindu usages and customs and thus became Hinduized unconsciously and without any objection by the Hindus. They in fact did not feel that the foreigners who came to India were people different from themselves any more than other tribes and castes in their own land. Thus the people of India did not feel the necessity for considering themselves socially separate from the rest of the world.

In India itself there were distinctions. The most important of them was the distinction of Varna. Those who belonged to one of the Varṇas considered themselves socially separate from those of the other. Whether there was any formal exclusion from a varna is doubtful, but there certainly was an exclusion from a caste; there was also exclusion from the twice-born circle; there were even tribes who were considered outside the four Varṇas. But these people differed from the Shūdras by imperceptible gradations as they do now.

More than this, the people in India for a long time did not have a conception of a society restricted to their own land. To a man living in the middle regions (the western part of the United Provinces), the barbarians in Deccan were no more near than the barbarians in Punjab, Afghanistan, Persia or Siam. The princes in the north intermarried with the princes in the south as well as with the princes belonging to the territory outside the present confines of India. The outlandish customs of the barbarians in Bactria, Persia, Kandahar and Punjab were abhorrent to the sacred people of the middle regions, but so were to them the customs of Bengal and Deccan. The dharma writers of the early days required the Āryas who lived in Madhyadesha to make atonement for migration into Deccan, Bengal, and Punjab, as the Hindus of to-day require it of those who go to Europe. Every man from one province going to another was a foreigner in that country, and incurred the taint of foreign emigration; it did not matter at all whether that province was located in Deccan, Bengal, Siam, Java, China, Tibet, Punjab or Persia.

In order to understand the lack of this Indian consciousness it is necessary to learn how a consciousness of a unity comes to a group of people. If all the people in a certain group have a tradition of common descent, then no other unifying element is necessary. But such conception generally exists in the case of very small groups of peoples. The different castes and tribes in India are examples of unities of this kind.

Besides the conception of unity of this kind there are other conceptions of unity produced by a different method. Political organizations also generate an idea of unity. Uniformity of customs and manners generates the conception, but it does not take root vigorously unless there is also a realization of contrast, separating the like from the unlike. People who worship the same god or adhere to the precepts of the same teacher begin to have a conception of unity. In this way the people who are living under the empire of a "religion" or "sampradāya" have a conception of unity. They begin to differentiate themselves from those who do not belong to the religion or sampradāya. As far as the Christian and Mohamedan peoples are concerned, they started their propaganda with a conception of their differentiation from other peoples, and of the unity of the persons of the same faith. In course of time the persons enclosed in the same fold increased in numbers, by taking in foreigners into the same fold. The conception of unity did not become larger, but the class of people enclosed in the group formulated by the conception became more widened, and remained definite. They had a conception of the difference between themselves and the other people, and the same has continued its existence. The nature of "religions" has been essentially one of separatism, and not of union. That is, societies living under a religion (sampradāya), whatever sympathy they may have for the members within the fold, essentially separate or at least try to separate the members from the unbelievers, inspiring into the members a spirit of unity within the fold and of distinction from the rest. When the fact is taken into consideration, the claims to cosmopolitanism, and unification which are often made by those who are living under a "religion," should sound satirical; but our ears being educated to hear such pretensions, they do not seem so ludicrous.

The spread of Hinduism has taken a different turn. A uniformity has been produced among the people of India who are called Hindus, but that uniformity is not a result of a conscious attempt to convert some portion of the people by the rest. When two tribes meet, each of the tribe borrows something from the other, and in course of time either the tribes fuse, or if they do not fuse at least a considerable uniformity is produced. When a number of tribes meet on the same spot, there is naturally a tendency towards uniformity of their customs and manners. The tribe that is dominant is imitated by the rest. The ideas of the different peoples tend to become uniform in the course of time; and if there be any class of people who are more intelligent and more cultured than the rest they are looked up to and are consulted by those who are less intelligent and less learned. If the families, clans or tribes which come together have certain distinctive gods of their own, some of the gods are forgotten and some others remain. The other gods when they are brought together either become special deities, subordinate to the supreme single deity, produced by the conception of the monotheistic philosophers in the tribes; or they may even be regarded by them as different manifestations of the same deity.

Thus by mere contact, by living together for a considerable period, are acquired a common stock of ideas, a common system of manners, a common tradition, a common theology, and a priestly caste; and when the tribes become more closely associated, the documents and the traditions of one tribe are regarded as a common heritage of the whole population. This has been essentially the process by which

Hinduism or the Hindu community and its traditions have grown. The chief factor which brought about the uniformity over a large track of area, has been the migration of the Brāhmaṇas and Brahmanized people everywhere, and the conquest of some parts of India by the recognized Brāhmanist princes.

This is the summary of events and processes that have been taking place for centuries. But these facts are such as cannot be easily observed by a foreigner, or even by an Indian. And for this reason there are some ideas and beliefs held and spread by ignorant men which have no ground whatsoever. Many people believe that the Hindus are the most conservative people, and haters of everything foreign, and that they do not include foreigners in their fold. Nothing can be further from the truth. Present Hinduism is nothing but a mixture of heterogeneous tribes and their traditions.[1]

But the reason why an inaccurate belief exists and is held

[1] I think that the late Sir Alfred C. Lyall is the first European who brought the facts regarding the Hinduization of "non-Hindu" tribes and several other interesting facts regarding "Brāhmanism" to the notice of the Western world. It would surely profit the reader to go over carefully his excellent article on "Missionary and non-Missionary Religions" in his *Asiatic Studies*, second edition, London, 1884. In fact, this whole book should never be neglected by the students of the Hindu social system. His essay mentioned above contains an idea which seems very curious to a Hindu reader. It says: "Qualified observers have thought that we might at any time witness a great Brāhmaṇic reforming revival in India if some really gifted and singularly powerful prophet were to arise among the Hindus." This passage shows how the European minds are fettered by the idea that for the progress of the people it is necessary for them to have a "religion" founded by one single prophet. Regarding the future of Hinduism and, in fact, the future of all communities enclosed in "religions," I have expressed my views further in this volume.

strongly by many people should also be explained. Every one sees Hindus becoming Mohamedans and Christians, but no one sees Christians or Mohamedans becoming Hindus. This observation leads an ordinary person to think Hinduism is an "exclusive" and a "national" "religion," while Christianity, Mohamedanism and Buddhism are "universal religions." Some persons believe that Hinduism is a "religion" which could appeal only to the people who are on the frontiers of civilization, and cannot appeal to persons professing "higher religions."

In order to explain why the above-mentioned inferences, though drawn from a correct observation, are erroneous, it would be necessary to explain many other primary conceptions. I have discarded the term "religion" as inapplicable to Hinduism. The essential difference between social systems like Hinduism and those social groups enclosed in religions like Christianity and Mohamedanism is, that in one case there is no conversion, that is, adoption of one group or individual by another, while in the other case there is. In one case the uniformity of manner, customs and beliefs are trusted to intercourse, intercourse itself is trusted to geographical proximity, and the increase of intercourse to time; while in the other, that is, in the case of society enclosed in "religion," an attempt is made to make the candidate for matriculation believe what members of the religion believe, and if he believes in the way they believe, and discards all that he has that may be different from their beliefs, then he is, individually, permitted in the social group enclosed by that religion. In this manner the religions, or rather the societies living under religions, have advanced and progressed. Hinduism is by no means "national," because all tribes in India were not completely Hinduized, that is, brought into contact with the civilized portion of the population, but many nations like Burma and Siam were brought under Hindu influence. For example, even to-day in Siam not only Buddha is respected and revered, but Indian heroes like Rāma are also revered, and I feel sure that if a number of Hindus go to Siam and become men of influence, it would be difficult in future to give a reason for separating the Siamese from the Hindus.

Thus considered in a true light, process of Hinduization is the only process of universal application. The process of uniting communities by " religions " has succeeded greatly, but, in future, the chances for such a process to do their work are doubtful. Would all Christians ever give up their " religion " and become Mohamedans or vice versa? Missionary work for the propagation of religion means propagation of antagonism and social conflict and not the promotion of any " universal religion."

But the process by which Hinduism is formed is capable of being carried to its logical extent. All civilizations are capable of being united into one civilization. There would be a stock of moral ideas common to all the world, which people would follow whether embodied in any scriptures or not. They will have some common ideas of God. The great teachers of mankind would be universally revered. All the religions in the world would hold the same status as the different sampradāyas hold in India. Religions would become tribal traditions, and Bible, Vedas and Koran would be looked upon as tribal documents, of merely historical interest. The respect for great teachers of mankind would not remain tribal but would become universal.

I have already said that there was no " Hindu consciousness" in India, and that there was no "Hindu dharma." To that I may add that there was no need for Hindu consciousness, and secondly, it was not possible that it should have come into existence.

There was no need for any Hindu consciousness because the tribes outside India and their civilization were capable of mixing easily with the people and civilization of India. As all the different tribes in India had exchanged their civilization and formed a common civilization, so with the meeting of other tribes in Central Asia, Hinduism would have become expanded and modified. Hindus had a larger social philosophy and social consciousness beyond the consciousness of tribe and varṇa. It was a "Mānava," or human consciousness. They were in fact developing a dharma for humanity, but this process was arrested by the rise of the two narrow heresies of semitic origin.

Of these two systems, the one which made its existence felt in India, first, is Mohamedanism.

When the Mohamedans came, they called all people who were in India, but who did not belong to Mohamedan religion, Hindus. The foreigners, at this time, had a "religion" of their own and their own priesthood. They not only denied the authority of the Vedas, but regarded Vedas themselves and other Hindu shāstras as heathen documents. To them the sacred Brāhmaṇa was nothing short of an infidel. All castes and tribes which did not acknowledge Mohamedan religion were Hindus. In Persian language, as I understand, Hindu means an infidel, unfaithful, black, and so forth. To Hindus and specially to Brāhmaṇas the Mohamedans were extremely impure. Mohamedans were noted for their cruelty, and are so even to-day, to a certain extent. The actions of cruelty, slaughter of cows by them, their disregard for Hindu gods, carried to the extent of breaking the temples and idols, their disrespect towards Brāhmaṇas, sharply differentiated them from the people in India. The people in India accepted the name Hindus and applied it to such as were not Mohamedans. To a Mohamedan, the word Hindu meant infidel, and to all the Hindus a Mohamedan was an individual of the impure species. As the Hindus began to think that all the people who did not belong to the Mohamedan religion were Hindus, the seed of Hindu consciousness was sown.

The Christians came later on the stage. Leaving aside the Nestorian Christians, whose influence on the early Indian society has not been studied, the Christian people who first landed in India and made their presence felt were the Portuguese. The attitude which the Portuguese adopted towards the Hindus was not very dissimilar from that adopted by the Mohamedans. And thus the Hindus sharply differentiated themselves from the Christians. When Hindus wanted to designate the Christians and the Mohamedans, they used the old classical terms like Hūṇa, and Yavana, expressive of cruelty, immorality and barbarism.

There are Parsis in India. There are some Jews also. But they were not sharply differentiated from the Hindus. Had the Parsis been disconnected from Persia, and had the Jews been cut off from the Jews in Europe, these two tribes would have become Hindu castes. They were, in fact, greatly Hinduized. Prior to the overthrow of the Maratha rule by the British, the Parsis used the Hindu ceremonies in their marriages, and even called the Brāhmaṇas to officiate. They abstained from killing cow and from the use of beef. Even the Jews had abstained from the slaughter of kine. The Jew and the Parsi women adopted the dress of Hindu women. Both the Jews and Parsis used to make vows before the Hindu gods, and would even help to build Hindu temples. Parsis had even translated their scriptures into Sanskrit.

If the distance between a Hindu and non-Hindu is not different in kind from the difference between two Hindu castes, why then should not the Hindus who become Christians be called Hindus, and Christianity and Mohamedanism Hindu sects? It is only because Christians and Mohamedans do not call themselves Hindus. A question may be asked, What, then, is the test by which a person can judge whether any particular sect or caste is Hindu or not? Does it depend entirely on the desire of the sect? Validity of claim to Hinduism to a great extent depends on the choice of the sect or tribe itself.

As the word "Hindu" is swinging between the social conception and religious or doctrinal conception, a person may make a narrow definition of Hindu and may exclude his sect or may make a broad definition and may include his sect, as he pleases. So a sect may class itself as a Hindu or non-Hindu according as it may or may not suit its policy, fancy, or prejudice. The little communities are time servers. Brahmos very often are heard contrasting themselves with Hindus, for social and political reasons, and very often to enable themselves to curse the "Hindu religion" and "Hindu superstition," so that they may have a chance of flattering their masters, the British Government, and the Englishmen in India. Very often Sikhs are classed as outside Hindus, specially by Englishmen,[1] and some

[1] The ignorant interpretation on the part of the Englishmen has led to one unfortunate result. Indian people believe that English-

Sikhs have imitated them out of ignorance. When Lord Morley gave a constitution to India and gave therein a special representation for Mohamedans, the Jains in Bombay Presidency came forward, and contrasting themselves with the Hindus demanded a separate representation.[1]

The most important test by which the place of a religious body or sect can be judged is, whether that sect is socially separate. Does a man who may join the sect lose his caste thereby ? Can people of that sect marry with Hindus who do not belong to that sect ? Do the members of that sect pollute Hindus ? If the sect is not separate in this sense, then the sect is a Hindu sect. At present Hindus who are not Sikhs intermarry with Sikhs. So Hindus of Gujrath who are not Jains intermarry with Jains, so these sects do not form a social body outside the Hindus. For the same reason Brahmos are a Hindu sect.

But some sects have practically become castes. In that case, the question whether a sect is Hindu or not can be decided by asking the following questions :—

(1) Does that sect adopt Hindu Gods ?

(2) Does that sect regard Brāhmaṇas as sacred ?

(3) Does that sect regard as sacred any of those works or documents which Hindus regard as sacred ?

men wish to create divisions in the people of India, for political reasons. They say this. Hindus think that Sikhs are Hindus; Sikhs think that they are Hindus; but Englishmen do not think so ! ! !

[1] Very similar has been the attitude of castes in the Maratha country, whose claim to be classed as Brāhmaṇas has not been generally admitted. Members of these castes, when among Hindus, are anxious to assert their claim to Brāhmaṇahood, but when they approach a European for a position, they generally give the popular name of their caste, and conceal the fact that they consider themselves as Brāhmaṇas, as there is a general impression that a Brāhmaṇa applicant is less likely to be favoured by the British.

(4) Was that sect founded by a man who was born a Hindu and who did not formally join any of the foreign religions ?

If with reference to a sect an affirmative answer to even one of the questions given above be made, then there is no reason for classing that sect as non-Hindu at present.

The Position of the Animists

A distinction is drawn by Europeans between Hindus and Animists. But Hindus themselves do not make any such distinction. The reason for this difference is due to the difference between the attitude of the European and of the Hindu towards the definition of a "Hindu" and "Hinduism." A European understands by the word "Hindu" a man who has certain kinds of notions and customs which are found among, and approved of by, the Hindus. Hindus define a Hindu as a man who has not fallen from Hinduism, that is, taken up the membership of any community like Christian or Mohamedan, which is not considered as a Hindu community.

The distinction between the Hindus and the Animists is thus based only on ignorance.

I may also add here that the distinction drawn between a Hindu and non-Hindu is merely a provisional one. It may change at any time. Hinduism may, in future, include Christians, Mohamedans, and Buddhists. Hinduism is an ever-changing society, which may expand and take in races and peoples irrespective of their religious beliefs. What societies it will absorb depends almost entirely on the circumstances, which cannot possibly be dwelt upon in this place.

CHAPTER IV

INTERNAL TIES

ALL Hindus, to-day, form a single community, at least in consciousness. Again, no person who is either a Christian or Mohamedan can be called a Hindu. A person who is formally converted to any of these religions is excluded from Hindu society. Though Hindus are thus separated from other religious communities, it should not be imagined that they are united by a bond of a common system of doctrines. There is, in fact, no system of doctrines, no teacher or school of teachers, no single god that is accepted by all the Hindus. Again no amount of deviation from the established doctrine, or disregard of any book, or even of some customs, would cause a person to fall from Hinduism; that is, become liable to exclusion from the Hindu community. The Hindu community may be compared to a faggot held together, not by any band that would bind all the sticks, but by a number of bands, every one of which would bind groups which are variously formed and overlap. Some of the sticks would be firmly bound in the faggot and others would be less so. If a stick breaks any of the bands that tie, it would still be bound by the rest, and would thus be kept bound within the faggot.

The ties which bind Hindus are many and varied. The most important of them are considered here.

The most important tie which binds most of the people together is, that they generally regard the Vedas as final authority. There is no single Hindu theophratry or caste which denies the authority of the Vedas, and attributes it to any other document. Even Gautama, the founder of Buddhism, did not deny the authority of the Vedas, and even pretended that his teachings were the pith of the Vedas, though his acquaintance with the Vedas was extremely superficial, and I personally doubt very much whether he had any acquaintance with the Vedas at all. For this attitude of Gautama towards the Vedas, Buddhism is considered by many, specially by Hindus, as a Hindu sect. From immemorial times there have been men, like Chārvākas, who denied the authority of the Vedas and even the existence of life after death. They would even say that the authors of the Vedas are liars and rascals. But such people did not attribute final authority to any other document. Moreover, such people have formed a very small minority, as they came mostly from the learned classes, probably from Brāhmaṇas.

Though the Vedas hold so high an authority, people who really read Vedas in India are an extremely limited minority. Among two hundred million Hindus, it is doubtful whether it would be possible to pick out ten thousand Hindus (that is, one in twenty thousand) who may have read even one or two Mandalas of the Rig-Veda in the original. Again, there are very few modern languages in India in which a complete translation of a single Veda, say Rig-Veda, would be available. At least, in Marathi, which is, one of the most important modern languages, there is no complete translation as yet made. The Vedas at present are more or less an arsenal whence are drawn arguments for philosophical and doctrinal controversy. Naturally, people do not look to the Vedas for actual moral and social guidance. Society is generally guided by the current moral ideas, whether incorporated in any scriptural work or not. The moral ideas in the community influence and are influenced by the ideas and practice of the higher classes. The moral ideas of the higher classes today are partially subject to the various Indian philosophies, partially due to the social and civil ideals as they may be reflected in the Indian writings on dharma, and in the European and modern Indian writings, specially of the evolutionary and utilitarian schools.

The spiritual life, that is sentiment towards divinities, is guided by compositions in Sanskrit and modern Indian languages, and by the ideas which those works generated or expressed. There are very few devotional hymns in Sanskrit of high character, excepting those in the Vedas addressed to forgotten Gods. The devotional songs abound in modern languages, which are considered as vernaculars, and they are not infrequently written by men of Shūdra Varṇa. To speak in incorrect but popular language, Sanskrit literature gives "religion" to philosophers, while common people derive their "religion" from the vernacular literature. In fact, most of the vernacular literature is devotional and semi-sacred, and came into existence only to save the people. In the Maratha country a great contribution to this vernacular literature is made by the Brāhmaṇas. These Brāhmaṇas were either apologetic or militant in their attitude for their innovation of writing in the vernacular.

"What, the Sanskrit language is made by God; has the Prakrit (the modern language, vernacular) come from thieves ?" Thus says Ekanātha in his introduction to the commentary on the eleventh book (Skandha) of Bhāgavata. Shrîdhara, a later writer, is much milder in his tone. He says, "Women do not understand the Sanskrit speech. To a person it (a work in it) is like sweet water in a deep well. How could this (water) be obtained by a weak person without rope and pail ? If he comes to a lake he will be able to quench his thirst at once ; so in order to save the weaker sex, God has created the works in the popular (Prakrit) language."

Thus it will be apparent that the significance of the Vedas to the Hindus is very different from the significance of the Bible to a Christian. Vedas are not, and are not expected to be popular. They are books which need be consulted only by scholars and philosophers, and so they are. It has been the policy of the Brāhmaṇas not to encourage the study of the Vedas by the masses, but to discourage it. The reason for this did not lie in a desire to cheat them, but only to prevent them from being misguided. Not only did they deny the Shūdra the right of studying the Vedas, but even to Brāhmaṇa pupils they taught the works only after the pupil had mastered dharma and other sciences. They think that, if a person without proper fitness reads the Vedas, he will be bewildered by the antiquated customs and moral ideas which abound in the Vedas.

Another reason why the study of the Vedas was discouraged by the Brāhmaṇas is that there had been a great revolution in the ideas of the Brāhmaṇas themselves. When I say that they discouraged the study of the Vedas, I mean that they discouraged the study of Mantras, and Brāhmaṇa portion of the Vedas only. They freely encouraged the study of the Upanishads. Even to-day it is customary among the orthodox Brāhmaṇas to stop reciting Mantras from the Vedas in the presence of a Shūdra, but they have no objection if the Shūdras listen to Upanishads. The revolution in ideas which is above referred to was this. There had been a change in the ideas of the nature of the divine being, of the use of animal sacrifices, the doctrine of vicarious suffering was abandoned, and the theories of Karma and transmigration of souls, which taught the man the necessity of suffering in his own person for his sins either in this or future lives, were promulgated. Though most of these ideas are discoverable in the later portion of Mantras and Brāhmaṇas, the spirit of these two portions of the Vedas was materially antagonistic to these new ideas. Under those conditions, it was necessary that the study of the Vedas by the masses should fall into disuse. Those books became documents fit to be studied by the philosophers only.

When any people cease to believe in any sacred, traditional work, they can discourage the use of the work only in two ways. They can call it a foolish and heathen document, or they may discourage its use or can prevent its study by the ignorant masses, and restrict it to philosophers only. The first course is possible only when the revolution in ideas takes place on account of the promulgation of some foreign creed, but when the new ideas or religions are of native growth, then they cannot brush aside the ancient document contemptuously. A parallel case can be quoted from modern occidental experience. Christianity was first started among the Jews, and thus the Old Testament became a sacred book. To-day many Christians do not believe in the ideas, doctrines and precepts of the Old Testament, or believe in it only so far as to explain the development of ideas which led to the formulation of Christianity. Under these circumstances we find many sincere Christian ministers who wish and frankly state that the Old Testament should not be taught to children or to persons who are not able to interpret or understand it in the "proper manner."

Another reason why they discouraged the study of the Vedas, is because they did not believe that its knowledge is necessary for salvation. They divided the Vedas thus: Mantra and Brāhmaṇa literature is called *Karma-Kānda*, the department of works; and the Upanishads is called the *Jñāna-Kānda*, the department of knowledge. According to latter-day ideas, salvation could be reached by knowledge alone, and therefore, what is necessary for the salvation of all people is knowledge, and this they did not keep out of the reach of Shūdras, women, or any other class of people. The *Karma* (Vedic rites) was regarded by them merely as a path to the attainment of knowledge, but they did not regard it as the only path. Many other paths, like worship and devotion (Upāsanā), were, according to them, equally valid.

Such were, in fact, the motives which led the early Brāhmaṇas to discourage the study of the Vedas in general and prohibit it to the Shūdras. To the Shūdras, though the Veda was prohibited, still Vedānta, the final knowledge, was never prohibited, but on the contrary recommended and preached. Shūdras on their part never felt the prohibition of the study of Vedas as a grievance, though to-day occasionally one hears a grievance of this kind, as some Christian missionaries make capital out of this by misrepresenting the real facts, either through ignorance or from the unworthy motives of alienating the Shūdra community from Hinduism.

Vedas cannot supply such moral ideas as would serve the needs of the society. For instruction in morals no Hindu would care to consult the Vedas, but he would turn his attention to Mahābhārata and to works on dharma and nīti.

To-day a Hindu receives instruction in the ideas of morality, in the distinction between good and bad, from his parents and from other elderly persons. He again gets acquainted with semi-sacred epics and Purāṇas, and principles of conduct which are inculcated by them. Philosophical theories regarding karma, transmigration of soul, etc., he generally absorbs from the society around him. If he reads any religious works at all it is not the Vedas but the Epics and Purāṇas, or, at least, the Gītā, in Mahābhārata. He generally reads the versions in modern languages, of these books.

Some Hindus again choose some particular spiritual teachers (Guru). These teachers have very often a very proud lineage extending over five or ten centuries. When the man selects his teacher in whom he may have confidence, that teacher acquaints him with the past series of his teachers. The teacher is supposed to see what stage of mind the pupil has reached and to advise him to follow a course of study or practices that may be fitted for him.

Those Hindus who are unable to read and write, as a large number of Hindus are, generally listen to the sacred works like Epics and Purāṇas from professional reciters. Many men again, literate or illiterate, commit to memory vernacular poems, which are either devotional or moral in their character. Such poems are very often written especially for the uneducated. They again know the lives and stories of saints and holy men, like Tukārāma,

Narsi Meheta and Namdeo, who are supposed to have attained salvation, either by their devotion or by self-sacrifice or by regard for truth.

But all these books like Epics and Purāṇas are supposed to be based on the Vedas and are supposed to contain nothing against the Vedas.

Vedas are generally consulted, when any question of social reform arises. Such has been the case since very early times; thus when the writer of the laws of Manu wanted to condemn any custom or practice he would say that it has no support of the Vedas. To-day, when the question of the validity of any custom arises, or the solution of any other doubtful point becomes necessary, an appeal to the Vedas is always made. With the advent of English education and Western ideas, the propriety of many current customs, like prohibition of the re-marriage of the widows, child marriage, prohibition of animal food, denial of the investiture of Maunji Bandhana, sacrament to women, and some other customs began to be questioned. Those who wanted to abolish the current customs began to appeal to the Vedas and said that modern Hindu customs like the ones given above have no Vedic authority; and advocated innovation on those grounds.

I have already said that books like the Epics and Purāṇas are supposed to be based on and to contain nothing against the Vedas; it should be remembered that it is only a theory. In fact, they contradict each other in various places. Still, the Epics (Itihāsas) and the Purāṇas are approved of by orthodoxy because those epics revere the Vedas. All that is expected of a writing which wishes to introduce any innovation, is that that writing should laud the Vedas or other traditional works highly and advise whatever may seem proper to the writer; and then the writing is sure to be approved of by orthodoxy. Under such circumstances the Epics, different dharma writings, and Purāṇas received authority among the people.

What relation do the later writings bear to the Vedas when they differ? The answer to this question at present cannot be given. The fault does not lie with any defect or difficulty of observation of facts. This question itself is yet to be fought out. There are various shades of opinion on this question. A large number of conservative men hold the view, that whatever may be proper in Vedic times is not necessarily proper now. This attitude is, of course, reasonable enough. But conservatism does not have any progressive principles in view when it speaks of the impropriety of applying the Vedic rules to modern society. It does not say that a society has a right to change customs to suit its needs. It asserts a doctrine like this. The people of the Vedic times were mighty and illustrious, while the men of to-day are frail. Though the Vedic sages performed some improprieties like eating beef, it may be proper for them, because those sages had a power to restore the cow to life. As we weak men of the Age of Discord (kali age) are unable to perform such miracles, we must not follow their example. Conservatism, in fact, upholds the principle that the later writings, like smṛitis, should be followed. They insist on this for another reason, viz., that the Vedas are too difficult to understand and the explanation of the Vedas by the sacred smṛiti writers should therefore be accepted. The social reformers who often appeal to the Vedas do so only because therein they generally find doctrines which support opinions which they approve of, and not out of a desire of restoring to the Vedas the authority which once belonged to them. No social reformer would be prepared to accept the Vedic manners as he finds them. A social reformer would certainly disapprove of the Levirate (Niyoga), which is supported by the Vedas, but which the later shāstras disapprove of. Still it must be admitted that the tendency of making the Vedas the final authority is becoming more and more marked. Some attempt is also made by theophratries like the Ārya Samāja to make Vedas popular. Still it is doubtful whether Hinduism is slowly tending more and more towards Vedism.

The facts may be reviewed and the relation of Vedas in the organization of Hindu society may be summarily stated as follows. The Vedas are more venerated than followed; what is actually followed is not the Vedas but such writings of sages as are not regarded antagonistic to the Vedas. Brāhmaṇical ritual is guided by the Vedas, and the Hindus generally regard Brāhmaṇas as their priests.

Besides the respect for the Vedas, the most important tie which binds all Hindus together is the common priesthood, the Brāhmaṇas. The priesthood in India is a hereditary endogamous caste, respected by all Hindus and considered as the head of the society. In fact, this is to a certain extent a far stronger bond than the Vedas. Though the religious ideas are not common and determinate, still the priesthood to which the Hindus owe their allegiance is determinate. The Brāhmaṇas again are firm in their position, irrespective of the opinion they hold.

Again, there has been an attempt in India for several centuries to regard the consensus of the opinion of the priesthood, and not the opinion of the Vedas, as the final authority. The Brāhmaṇas, of course, do not take a defiant attitude towards the Vedas, but simply present themselves as interpreters of the Vedas and of the tradition. The reasons why Hindus prefer to be guided by the Brāhmaṇas instead of by a direct appeal to scripture are very plain. Unlike those of the Christian theophratry the scriptures of the Hindus are bulky, and extremely difficult to interpret with regard to the tradition, and it is more convenient to follow the opinions of the specialists in such matters. Moreover, the Brāhmaṇas have not been merely the directors of ritual but also teachers and guides in temporal matters, like law, custom, and in proper procedure as determined by various sciences, like medicine and astrology. They would advise their client with reference to temporal success as well as worship, e.g., on matters like proper time for sowing seed, ploughing land, building house, and on various questions connected with marriage and education.

How did the Brāhmaṇas make themselves indispensable? How did they secure the confidence of the Hindu community? These questions demand a long historical discussion which I am not prepared to enter into in this place. I shall treat them fully in a separate monograph which I expect to publish on the rise of the priesthood. But I give here one essential of the process. It is this. The Brāhmaṇas would assert that the knowledge of the dharma depends on the knowledge of the Shāstras (sciences). That is, the explanation of what duty is depends on the distinction between what is good and what is bad. What is good or proper to do is something which should be ascertained by an appeal to sciences (Shāstras). Whilst they admitted the Vedas as the source of dharma, they also asserted that the Vedas cannot be properly interpreted or understood, unless they are interpreted by men learned in sciences. Thus the Brāhmaṇas superseded the Vedas by the sciences. As the Brāhmaṇas themselves represented the sciences, it became necessary for a layman to consult the Brāhmaṇas, regarding the advice of science (Shāstra) on matters which may concern him. Again, unlike the Christian scriptures, the Hindu scriptures were never claimed to be the complete guides in science. All the rules of dharma were never claimed to be discovered, and so there was always a scope for addition. Many orthodox Brāhmaṇas to-day assert that dharma can never be completely known. This attitude is perfectly consistent with the fact that all the sciences on which the knowledge of duties (dharma) depends are held to be incomplete.

Another reason why the Brāhmaṇas' authority remained so universally recognized in India is that their position has never been uncertain. It has always been at the top. Buddhism tried to dethrone them, but tried in vain. In political revolution, castes, tribes and families rise and fall, to and from kshatriyahood, but the Brāhmaṇas have remained unmolested. The tribe or family that may become dominant had to approach and flatter the Brāhmaṇas to get its own status as kshatriyas recognized.

Though respect for the Vedas and the Brāhmaṇas joins a large number of communities, their hold has not been complete. A large number of castes and tribes have neither the right to read or listen to a Veda, nor the right of approaching the Brāhmaṇas to minister to their own needs. Their priestly function is performed either by priests of the same caste or by some inferior caste. Still, these castes cling to Hindu society and are regarded as a Hindu caste, though they hold in the community a low position.

Of other strings which bind them to Hindu community the following are important—

(i) First of all, as far as impure classes are concerned, though the Vedas and the service of the Brāhmaṇas are beyond their reach, these classes still have a religious respect for them. They regard Brāhmaṇas as sacred, because the castes which they look up to hold them so. They also regard the Vedas as sacred books, and also regard themselves as unlucky mortals who through their impurity have no right for the Vedas.

(ii) Though the Shūdras and the impure classes have no right to read the Vedas, still they have a right to read or listen to Purāṇas and other sacred works, which are mainly written in vernacular languages, which are based on the Vedas.

(iii) As these lower castes read the Purāṇas they believe in and worship the same deities, like Rāma, Kṛishṇa, Shiva, Durgā, as the higher castes do. Both higher and lower castes have common festivals, which are connected with these deities.

(iv) Again, most of the castes have the same beliefs as the higher castes have; those beliefs are numerous and they occupy various areas. The beliefs which are most common are those relating to the laws of transmigration of soul, and of karma.

(v) Again, some kind of tradition regarding origin connects them with the Hindu society in general. A large number of castes trace their descent from some god or sage mentioned in the Hindu mythology.[1] Some castes trace their origin from some well-recognized dominant Hindu caste. If a caste occupies a low position there is a story current in that caste, explaining what high caste they once belonged to, and what actions or calamities caused their downfall. The story may give some historical causes or some mythical causes; by the latter I mean causes which attribute their downfall to the anger of some god.

Besides these various ties, there is another intended to unite together not only all Hindu castes but the entire world. That tie is the Hindu philosophy itself, which is quite cosmopolitan in its nature. It is the expectation of the writer that the principles of this philosophy, though now dormant on account of the political insignificance of the Hindus, will ultimately triumph and will bring the entire world together. Those cosmopolitan principles of philosophy are these—

The most important feature of the Hindu cosmopolitanism is the pantheistic theology. When I say pantheistic I should not be understood to say that the Hindus are not monotheists. In fact Hindu philosophy teaches monotheism in the most uncompromising manner. Some European writers have contrasted pantheism and monotheism, but in my opinion monotheism and pantheism should be regarded as synonyms, and pantheism is the only possible form of any consistent monotheism. The Hindu pantheistic creed is this—

---

[1] I have used the word *mythology* because it is used by the earlier European writers. According to the Hindu notion the stories which are called mythology by Europeans are nothing short of history. The Sanskrit words are Itihāsa and Purāṇa, i.e., history and antiquity.

There is but one Being, no second; nothing really exists but the universal spirit called Brahman, and whatever appears to exist is mere illusion. That Brahman which is the one sole, self-existing supreme and all-pervading Self (Ātman), the only existing Essence, the one eternal germ of all things, delights in infinite expansion, in infinite expansion of itself, in infinite creation, dissolution, and re-creation through infinite varieties, and diversities of operation. Hence all visible form is an emanation from God, and hence, to begin with, the lowest visible objects—water, wood, and stones, birds, beasts and men; these are but steps in the infinite evolution of his being. Hence, also, a series of higher forms of existence such as demigods, good and evil spirits, inferior gods, superior gods, is traceable upwards in an ascending scale from man. All these men, gods or demigods, start from, and end in, the same essence.

As Hindus held a pantheistic theory of the nature of god, a fight for the propagation of that god worshipped by a particular tribe is meaningless to them. They tolerated idolatry frankly and openly. Idolatry is in fact nothing more than a representation of the abstract by the concrete, of remote by proximate, and of the principal by the agent. It is in fact possible for a very small class of people to conceive of abstract conception of God, and the writer may well express his own scepticism regarding the existence of any man on earth who can conceive of infinities like time, space or God with the same vividness as that of a finite object.

All worship, according to the pantheistic doctrine is due to the reverence of some great power manifested. As people conceive of God only by manifestations, it is but natural that they should worship some particular manifestation and that their idea of God should be partial and finite. It is folly to be proud of particular revelation or manifestation, for the infinite being is capable of being partially manifested at any place or to any people, but a true philosopher should rise above all the partial manifestations. He should free his intellect from idolatry and bibliolatry, but may still continue to practise the meaningless forms of worship through of no use to him, so that the less intellectual classes who may imitate philosophers may not quit the worship and prayer too early. On this subject the theory expounded by Sureshvarāchārya is this—

Those who have attained the " recognition of the Self (ātmajñāna) may continue their adherence to the various instruments (sādhana) and paths like worship and prayer, intended only to lead an individual to the final knowledge. The difference between the conditions prior and posterior to the attainment of knowledge is this. In the former case the actions like worship and prayer are helpful instruments to an individual, but in the latter case they are merely reflex actions due to the prior accumulation of training and are meaningless and are unprofitable to the individual himself.

The attitude of the philosopher towards an ignorant person, and his worship ought to be tolerant. What a philosopher is expected to do is not to advocate a new god or document for the acceptance of the people, but to raise the ignorant mind from concrete to abstract conception of divinity. To a Hindu philosopher what name you give to God is immaterial, because any name is equally foolish on account of the finiteness of the word itself. The statement would become clearer if I draw upon the custom. When a student approaches a teacher for advice regarding the nature of god and the desirable attitude towards him, what a teacher does is to ask the student what his favourite god or goddess is. After learning it from the student as to his favourite god, the teacher explains to him that the idea which he has of that god is not correct. The teacher then teaches him some verses regarding that particular deity which describe the deity not according to the idea which the student may have by listening to many stories from "history and antiquity," but give him a Vedantic idea where that particular deity may be identified with Brahma. The teacher then tries to get out of the pupil's mind the popular idea of god, and tries as far as possible to make him feel his union with the Absolute. This process of instruction is called Brahma-bodhana.

After this Brahma-bodhana has been attained by the student, the student continues to worship the same god as the ignorant does, but his attitude in the worship is entirely different. He simply conforms to the custom, though the ceremonies and the idols are meaningless to him. He does not have hatred for the idols as the ignorant monotheist has; for the idols and everything else in the world are but one entity, Brahma. The student very often repeats the same hymns and same verses as the unintelligent, but he sees a different meaning. In Hindu literature, Sanskrit as well as vernacular, there are a large number of poems descriptive of various gods. Apparently these descriptions conform to the idea of the finite gods of "the history and antiquity" (Epics and Purāṇas) but to a man who has received what is called "the key of the teacher" (Guru–Killi) the meaning would seem entirely different. There are some verses which are called "riddles" which give absurd and inconsistent descriptions regarding the god, but those who have received the key of the teacher will see a meaning entirely different in it. Let me give a translation of very common Marathi verses of Jñanadeva of the thirteenth century.

"God Viṭṭhala quarrelled with his consort Rakhumai, and who will now put a stop to their quarrel? It is I, Jñanadeva, humble at the feet of Nivṛitti (elder brother and teacher of Jñanadeva) will do it."

The meaning of the above verses is not so simple. The names, Viṭṭhala, Rakhumai are to be interpreted as Brahma and Māyā; and the names Nivṛitti and Jñanadeva are to be taken as common nouns, meaning renunciation and knowledge respectively. We shall then have the verse to mean: "The sole eternal one Self is always in conflict with Māyā, which causes all the delusion, and makes one thing appear different. Who will stop this conflict? It is knowledge alone which leads to renunciation." Suppose a man of the Christian caste goes to a Hindu teacher for spiritual elevation, the teacher would then tell him how different is the real Christ from the Christ whom he really adores. The teacher would persuade the student to ignore the historical Christ as the latter is only a partial manifestation of the real Christ, omniscient and everlasting, incorporated in human form and acting in human ways. Thus the chief object of the teacher is not to create a change in the object of worship, but in ideas and philosophy, leaving the old paraphernalia unchanged.

Another characteristic of Hindu cosmopolitanism is the recognition of the propriety of the various forms of worship. In this way they got over the differences which the dissimilarity of worship may have caused among the various tribes and sects. Above the practice of the variety of worship they had a philosophy which discouraged the oppositions and reconciled the contradictions. It is necessary to recall here some more of their philosophical tenets.

To the Hindus who believe in the Vedānta philosophy, the highest aim of life is to be united with Brāhma. This Brāhma, the one universal essence, is to the external world what yarn is to the cloth, what milk is to the curds and to butter, what earth to a jar and what gold is to ornaments made thereof. This Essence is both creator and creation, actor and act. Nothing really exists in the world without Brāhma. It is our ignorance which prevents us from seeing the real unity of all the objects in the world through the various diversities. As the consciousness and the pride of our individuality is nothing but an inadequate appreciation of the unity, it is the aim of life to realize that unity thoroughly by merging ourselves into the one universal and eternal essence.

The end of all sciences according to the Hindu philosophy is the realization of the unity of everything that exists. Realization of this final truth is "the knowledge." The knowledge of God and the union with him is nothing else. Evidently that knowledge is salvation and the object of human life.

It has been the dogma of the orthodox philosophy that salvation could be reached by "knowledge" alone. Though the Hindus of the various schools of thought and religions (sampradāya) admitted this principle, it did not prevent them from devotion, vow worship or sacrifice, for they also held, that the required knowledge could not be reached at once, as persons who could be able to acquire that knowledge easily would necessarily be few. Very few are the people who will be able to cross the obstacle of "ignorance" with the speed of the bird (Vihangamamārga), but most are able to pass over the obstacle by the slow but steady course of the ant (Pipī-likā-mārga). The end (knowledge) is necessary of achievement, but what method may be adopted to attain that end is immaterial. As the methods to be adopted, to explain a certain problem, vary in accordance with the capability of the student, there is no single necessary procedure (sādhana) for the attainment of the highest knowledge and therefore of the eternal bliss. Man may go by any path which may suit his intelligence or temperament. Whatever path he goes by, he will reach the same place ultimately; that is, he will acquire the necessary knowledge and thus reach salvation. Every effort made towards obtaining eternal bliss is valuable whatever it may be. All forms of worship and discipline, whether it be vows, study, meditation, devotion, sacrifices, resolutions, austerities or self-torture, assist a man in his progress.

Hindu philosophy regarded all kinds of "instruments" (like worship, technically called *sādhana*) as permissible, but from this it should not be inferred that they held one instrument or path as good as another. The missionary spirit of the Hindus is displayed here. Unlike the followers of the "religions," the Hindus did not advertise any God or philosopher of their tribe. All that they cared to show to a person is a better and an easier path. A Hindu "teacher" (Guru) is primarily the "shower of the path" (Mārga-darshaka). Some teachers may know how to lead a student to knowledge by the path of devotion, while some teachers may be able to initiate intelligent students to the path of knowledge directly. But every teacher considers it his duty to lead his student if he can beyond the finite conception of God. The missionary spirit of the Hindus is not directed to attack the traditional god of the tribe they come in contact with, but to let the tribe worship their god or gods in their own way, but with an enlarged conception, and to admonish the members of that tribe that the god who has manifested himself partially to that tribe is in reality very different, more powerful than they conceive, that it is the duty of a man to know His real nature, and that there are higher forms of worshipping him than what the tribe may be practising.

Another aspect of the Hindu cosmopolitanism has been the exaltation of the principle of duty (dharma) above everything else. Whether a man is a theist or a chārvāka (an atheist) he has to follow dharma. This dharma is eternal and infinite. To whatever tribe a man may belong, of whatever sampradāya (religion) he may be a disciple, whatever school of thought like Dvaita or Advaita he may follow, of whatever class he may be, he has to follow the *dharma*. They separated the dharma entirely from mata (doctrine regarding god) or mārga (path to worship god). The duties of man were separated from worship and conceptions of God. They demanded of a man not worship but fulfilment of his duty.

The moral of the philosophy is this. It is not a matter of importance as to what god a person worships, what doctrine he believes, what path he follows, provided he follows dharma, the duties of man, as a man, and those of his position assigned to him either as a teacher, warrior or a trader. Every man is expected to be Dhārmika, that is, dutiful.

This is the general attitude which brought all the castes and tribes, their worships, their beliefs, under one system.

There is nothing tribal in this philosophy; it is capable of universal expansion ; it was intended to be so. According to Hindu ideas, it is perfectly proper, or even necessary for a Christian to follow his tribal customs, provided he follows mãnava-dharma, his duties as a man.

Let us now see how those principles which have united the various races, their cults and traditions under Hinduism have operated in the land of the rising sun, and helped to unify the various peoples and the beliefs in the land and have prepared them for the unification of the world's culture.

Leaving the influence of the Western civilization aside, Japan had been subjected mainly to two influences. The primitive beliefs and cults in Japan were influenced first by the Chinese culture and secondly by the Indian culture, through the medium of the Chinese and Korean teachers. A careful study of these influences will give us the principles of the unification of cultures and we shall see that those principles were the same which led to the formation of Hinduism and were given by India to Japan.

We have no definite knowledge as to where the Japanese come from. We do not know also what different strains have produced the modern Japanese ; still the fact that a variety of strains and tribes have produced the modern Japanese is something well proved. Their earliest conception of God was " something superior," and it is in this sense that their word " Kami " is to be interpreted in the earliest records. The objects of worship, then, were the marvels of nature, its processes, its powers, its fertility, its ways of reproduction, its awe-inspiring mountains and seas and heavenly bodies and sky, trees, beasts, birds, great fishes, reptiles, and the reproductive powers of man, all of which were mysterious, wonderful, connected with our weal or woe. They expected to please these superiors with prayers for happiness and for escape from evil, and with offerings like the fruits of the field, the spoils of the chase, the leaves of trees, the works of one's hands, pieces of cloth, intoxicating liquors, and in greater stress of danger by the horse, the sword and the wife.

Japan emerged out of this primitive character of worship and theology by the touch of the Chinese civilization. Sometimes in the dim past, probably after the Christian era, one tribe coming from the south-western part of what is now Japan spread itself all over the country and made itself master after strenuous fighting extending perhaps over generations. Some time after this conquest and political unification of the tribes, Chinese literature and civilization were introduced. For centuries preceding the eighth a twofold process was going on: acquaintance with the continental culture and consolidation of the Empire.

The Chinese civilization had not only an elaborate theory of government, but a cosmogony and a philosophy. This higher civilization came into contact with the primitive civilization of Japan, and this contact led to some very important results.

The Japanese did not accept the Chinese civilization in wholesale, but accepted it in such a manner as to suit their needs. The Chinese thought was accepted in the main and was used to systematize the local traditions. The different legends of various growths were retold with some principle at the basis. The old legends and traditions were not annihilated, as is usual in the migration of "religions," but preserved. The Chinese philosophy added to Japanese traditions a theory and conscious explanation and system.

The Chinese philosophy which was introduced into Japan and which systematized the ancient myths and traditions, was not used to help them in further theological speculation, the cosmology was not prepared for its own sake, but was prepared with the object of serving the polity. "Thus in this (*Records of Ancient Matters*) so called 'Bible of the Japanese' we have a work written with a definite purpose, the correction of false claims and the establishment of the monarchy, while in a secondary way we are to be given the origin of the universe itself. There is no pretence of a religious motive, nor of setting forth a moral code, but, in accordance with Chinese precedents, Japan too shall have a cosmology, a national history, and an account of the fashion in which the imperial house obtained its power." [1]

The influence of the Chinese philosophy helped Japan to unify its cults to some extent, but the influence of Indian thought and method was greater in this direction. Japan was thoroughly changed by the influence of Buddhism. But the Buddhism which influenced Japan was entirely different from what was preached by Gautama. It was in fact Hinduism which was carried to Japan under the name of Buddha. As Hinduism absorbs all heterogeneous worships and rites, so did the Greater Vehicle sect of Buddhism. In the year 552 A.D. priests and images migrated to Japan, but the foreign cult instead of destroying the pre-existing cult absorbed it. One Japanese Buddhist, Kobo-Daishi, who was a man of great influence, declared that the native Gods were incarnations of Buddha himself. As in India the pantheistic Vedanta philosophy united all divinities and worships instead of annihilating them, so in Japan; Shinto was not deserted, but was turned to account by Buddhism.

[1] Knox, *The Development of Religions in Japan*, 1907, p. 57.

Thus the Indian system became the authorized interpreter of the old. The Indian system simply gave them new knowledge and thus united all the various pre-existing cults.

I say that it was Hinduism which united the worships of Japan because the doctrines which bound Japan together are the very things which Gautama opposed. All that had been exorcised came back again. The doctrine of the essential unity of the Self (Ātman) was never preached by Gautama. Thus Buddhism would have lost the all-absorbing power which is so essential a characteristic of Hinduism, had not his followers furtively returned to the great theories of Vedanta philosophy. This underhand deal was transacted according to the following method.

The place of Brahma in the Vedanta philosophy was taken by Buddha in the Buddhistic philosophy. Buddha himself was identified with the Absolute. The figure of the historic Buddha was kept, but it was greatly modified. The historic Buddhas were represented to be many, but were regarded as all one in the invisible being of the infinite. Thus the historical Gautama occupied a subordinate place, since a way was opened for beliefs in many Buddhas and salvation in Nirvāna is replaced by the desire for the attainment of Buddhahood and absorption in the absolute. Buddhism did not remain merely a system of the teaching of Buddha, but a system leading the followers to be re-absorbed in the absolute through a number of stages which lead to the absolute; and in the series of stages "the Perfect one" was supposed to have reached the highest stages.

The fate of Gautama's teachings should not lead us to draw a conclusion that the original good doctrine was corrupted by unworthy followers. A charge of this kind is often made against the followers of Buddha and Jesus. In fact the case was entirely different. One of the characteristics of the life of great teachers like these is that their teachings are merely occasional utterances. Such utterances are very rarely consistent, and the task of making them consistent falls on their followers. In this particular case Gautama himself is responsible for all the further grotesque development of his doctrine. He was by no means a man of good education, when judged even by the standard of his times. He had a great deal of antipathy towards all sciences and speculations. How great an antipathy he had towards all sciences can be proved from his dialogues. To him medicine, astronomy and other sciences were low; and Gautama prided himself on being free from them. He condemned Brāhmaṇical sciences and philosophy by a sophistry of the following type: "This philosophy," he would say, "is based on experience; experience is contact of objects and senses; this contact creates 'craving,' and craving leads to re-birth, that is to all sorrows of the world."

Another reason why Buddhism returned again to the doctrines of Vedanta rejected by their teacher is, that the only possible form of consistent monotheism is pantheism as taught by Vedanta. All forms of theistic thought would ultimately be driven to the Vedantic doctrines, or suffer inconsistency. Indian scholars and philosophers have experienced this for centuries, and have therefore called the system of thought "Vedanta," or the ultimate bound of knowledge.

In the process of universal cosmopolitanism a great disturbing element has been the rise of some sampradāyas or religions. They once created some disturbance in India, but to-day principles of dealing with them have been formulated, and the evils they used to cause are tending to disappear. The future native sampradāyas are not likely to cause much social disturbance; but the foreign sampradāyas like Christianity and Mohamedanism will give a great deal of trouble for years to come; but they also will yield to the process, which has eliminated the evil effects of various native religions within Hinduism. For the comprehension of the situation it is necessary to dwell on the relation of sampradāyas in Hinduism.

I repeat here that Hinduism is not a religion; Christianity or Islam bears no similarity to it, but they resemble in character the various sampradāyas in India. European writers translate the word sampradāya by the word "sect." But the word ought to be translated by the word "religion," or more properly by the word theophratry, which I am using in this work. The relation which the sampradāyas bear to Hinduism is the same as that which Christianity and Mohamedanism bear to the entire world.

The word sampradāya is used in the sense either of a religious society or of the doctrines of the society.

Sampradāyas, in the first sense, are societies established by a particular religious leader after whom they are named. These sampradāyas were generally started by men who were dissatisfied with some tenets of the philosophy of their times, and who believed that salvation can be achieved by a better and an easier path, and wanted to make it accessible to other men by showing them the path. These teachers would preach and make disciples; the society which is thus formed becomes a sampradāya, provided that it can ensure any permanence.

These sampradāyas generally regard their founder as

a specially inspired man; or some semi-divine being; or at least men with knowledge far superior to that of ordinary men.

These sampradāyas very often become social groups distinct from the rest. All the men in a sampradāya become brothers, at least theoretically, and become separate from the people outside the sampradāya. Intermarriage between the members in the sampradāya and outside the sampradāya tends to cease, specially when they attack the caste system openly, or create some great disturbance in the existing social arrangements. The result is that the sampradāya becomes a caste distinct from the other castes.

These sampradāyas are missionary in their character. As these societies wish to increase their membership as much as possible, they become in fact, "Open-door Castes." Very often they become the dumping ground of the refuse of all caste, that is, immoral women, and other excommunicated and ostracized persons.

In the sampradāyas founded by the latter-day sages one of the most noticeable features has been the exaggeration of the principle of faith and love (bhakti), so that even caste within the sampradāya was subordinated to it. Devotion to Kṛishṇa (Vishṇu) or Shiva, especially an enthusiastic love for the former, become a bond of union stronger than all social distinctions. In some parts of India they tended to create new religious castes.

These sampradāyas attracted people of inferior mental calibre, specially "women and shūdras." The reason for this is not that a Brāhmaṇa has been too great an aristocrat to join a levelling sect; Brāhmaṇas kept aloof because to them devotion being an inferior "instrument" (sādhana), did not appeal, and because of other reasons which will be explained later.

The separatist tendencies of the sampradāyas are less marked in some than in others. In some cases the sampradāyas become practically endogamous tribes, while other sampradāyas are very loose associations.

One cannot say that these sampradāyas did much good to India. The general policy of the Brāhmaṇas towards the sampradāyas had been that of disapproval and hostility, when these sampradāyas tended to disturb the social organizations. Persons gifted with the skill of offering easy and popular solutions attribute the Brāhmaṇical attitude to the Brāhmaṇas' love for caste system and to his religious intolerance; but nothing could be farther from truth. Brāhmaṇas have in fact never shown any particular fondness for caste system as it has been existing. They, on the contrary, have always tried to bring the caste system to a more reasonable condition. Many of the charges against the Brāhmaṇas trace their origin to error and mendacity on the part of the ignorant and the inimical. Brāhmaṇas have, in fact, clearly realized that the sampradāyas do not destroy caste system but merely promote it.

To a society it is highly injurious that some members should organize a tribe on the unstable foundation of some theological doctrine, or love for some teacher, and create social anarchy for the advantage of the tribe. Intolerance towards any sampradāya or religion should be carefully distinguished from intolerance towards the heterodoxy of thought. The attitude of the Brāhmaṇas, and in fact of all orthodox Hindus, has been to encourage the freest discussion and to tolerate the greatest diversity of thought, regarding morals, aims of life, and the nature of divinity, but to discourage those heresies which disturb the social order by creating of new religious tribes.

Resemblance between religion and sampradāya and the difference between a sampradāya and a sect may be shown in another way. To-day, if you ask a large number of Hindus as to whether they are followers of any particular sampradāya, they will answer in the negative. A European or American will be able to answer the question whether he is Methodist, Baptist, Catholic or Presbyterian. Similarly in India any man belonging to any sampradāyas would be able to tell what division of sampradāya he belongs to. A Vaishṇava can tell you whether he is a Nimbārka or Rāmānuja, a Jain can tell you whether he is a Shevetāmbara or a Dāgambara a Brahmo can say whether he is an Adi Brahmo or Nūtana Brahmo. People who are followers of any sampradāya can always tell any particular sampradāya that they follow. When the sampradāya divides itself, by an introduction of schism, some members go one way, some the other. When any sampradāya takes in all the people of any particular locality, we find that every man there will profess to be a follower of the sampradāya, and a member of the particular sect therein. The same rule can explain why almost every man in Europe or America can tell what sect he belongs to.

It has been the ideal of Hinduism to discourage the sampradāyas, and to promote dharma eternal and infinite. As intelligence and education advance in India the sampradāyas fall into disuse, and when education declines the sampradāyas multiply. These sampradāyas were multiplying among unintelligent classes, and they increased considerably during the Mohamedan régime.

What service do the sampradāyas or religions do ? They tend to destroy the old social distinctions and create new ones. They take individuals from different tribes and castes and create new tribes and castes, based on worship or theological doctrine. A man who becomes, for example, a Mahānubhāva or Lingavat (Lingāyat) loses his caste and becomes a member of the caste of Lingāyats or Mahānubhāvas. But even in this process the old caste distinctions are not entirely obliterated. Even those Hindus who join the sampradāya of Christ or the Christian religion are proud of lineage from a high Hindu caste.[1] These sampradāyas do one distinct service: those people from low caste, who cut off their relations with their own low caste by joining a sampradāya, gain in status. They lose the old status connected with the caste and gain the status gained by the sampradāya. A Mahāra who belongs to a Mahānubhāva sampradāya finds his status raised thereby; the same case happens if that Mahāra becomes a Christian.

Will these sampradāyas ever succeed in breaking the old social orders? I think not. The sampradāya system (the religion system) of social organization has its weak points.

The sampradāyas which take recruits from the lowest castes degrade themselves in the social hierarchy. This law is true of societies of all kinds and of all localities. I have seen in the college fraternities in America that if any fraternity take the Jews in, the fraternity itself is lowered in status. The Jews seem to be conscious of the above-given law. Even though they occasionally make "converts" from the Christian people, it seems very doubtful whether they would extend the membership of the tribe

[1] I have known various cases where Hindus who join the caste of Christians are averse to marriages with those Christian families who were Mohamedans prior to the conversion. I have also seen that Christians whose forefathers were of Mahāra caste would find it almost impossible to get girls from the Christian families of Brāhmaṇa descent.

to the negroes. The admission of persons of low status to a body whether religious or social, always tends to pull down the body in the public eyes. This fact is keenly appreciated by the sampradāyas, and many of them to-day show some aversion to admit persons of the lowest caste to the fold. The sampradāya of Christ has the same difficulty to overcome. As the Christian religion draws most of its recruits from the lowest caste, the Christian caste itself is often called by the name of the lowest caste.[1] The *de facto* status of the Christian caste to-day is not the lowest, but the next above the lowest. The man from the lowest caste who joins this sampradāya gains in status, while the man from any of the higher castes loses by joining it.

Comparing the two types of castes, the old tribal caste, and the religious castes, we find that each has some advantage which to-day the other does not possess.

Those who join sampradāyas are brothers, but with them the feeling of democracy and brotherhood is not quite so strong as it is in the older caste. A Brāhmaṇa, however poor he may be, is equal of any other Brāhmaṇa, even if the latter is a millionaire. No Brāhmaṇa of a high rank would be at all ashamed to marry the daughter of a Brāhmaṇa cook. The same strong feeling of democracy exists in other castes also.

The advantage which lies with the sampradāyas is this. They have the capability to expand, they admit members from other castes into their own. If this spirit of expansion of a caste by the absorption of foreign elements could be infused into castes, then a great deal of trouble, due to the caste system, would disappear.

[1] Many ignorant people in the Maratha country, when they see any person become a Christian, say that he has become a Mahāra.

CHAPTER V

MEMBERSHIP OF HINDUISM

THE manner in which the different groups and castes are federated together under Hinduism has already been stated. The question that now comes before us is how a man who is not born a Hindu can become a Hindu and how he can disconnect himself from Hinduism.

There has been great ignorance on this matter in the European world. This ignorance is displayed by the phrase, "Conversion to Hinduism." Europeans who are in the habit of thinking in their own terms, find Hindu customs very difficult to comprehend. In Europe conversion to a religion means two things. First, the man who is converted to a religion is supposed to hold ideas similar to the rest of the people of that religion. Secondly, he joins the society of those who hold a similar belief. A Jew who becomes a Christian forsakes connexion with his own tribe and joins the tribe of the Christians.

On account of this state of affairs the Western people are led to adopt the two conditions as essentials of conversion, namely: (i) Conversion to ideas should be formally expressed by a ceremony like baptism; (ii) The conversion to ideas should be followed by adoption of the convert by the society which holds those ideas. The underlying belief of the western people is that similarity of belief and formal adoption thereof should open the doors of the community. This principle has not been accepted by Hindu society to any large extent. Mohamedans have followed this principle zealously, Christians are following it to a large extent, though nowadays they are showing a tendency to give this principle up. As Hindus do not uphold this principle generally, the question of a formal conversion to Hinduism does not exist.

Membership of Hindu society is not dependent on the opinion which a person may hold. It is a privilege restricted to those who are born of members. No amount of similarity of opinion would make an Englishman or a Frenchman a Hindu.

It should not be supposed that Hindus do not have a missionary zeal. They have it, and they display it. The missionary zeal of a Hindu is directed to propagate the ideas which they hold. If conversion simply means making other people hold the same ideas as one may hold, Hindus have made converts, are anxious to make converts, and will continue to make converts. But if conversion means extension of the membership of one's own social group, Hindus have not shown any great zeal, and are not likely to show such zeal for years to come.

Though Hindus have closed the doors of their own society to non-Hindus, there are many exceptions to that rule. The fact is that Hindus do not let anybody come in by the front door, but they do not have an objection if anybody comes in by the back door.

Under the empire of Hinduism there are a number of sampradāyas (religions) like Sikhism, Mahānubhāva sect, Ārya-samāja, Brāhmo-samāja and others, which make proselytes from peoples who are considered as outside the

Hindu society. These sects have, in fact, become tribes, socially separate to a certain extent, but not entirely. These religions have shown a tendency towards expansion, and the most noted of them is the Ārya-samāja. They do some missionary work, and as far as Ārya-samāja is concerned, every member of it is practically a missionary. Christians or Mohamedans who join these theophratries come from two classes: (i) some people become converted to this sect because they believe in the doctrines; (ii) in a number of cases when a Hindu wishes to marry a Christian woman, who is generally an Englishwoman, he gets her converted into that sect and marries her. These converts become members of these sampradāyas, religiously and socially, and therefore they also become members of the Hindu community.

The underlying principle is this: any caste considered as a Hindu caste has a right of determining who should be included as members. The Hindu community as a whole has nothing to do in this matter. Sympathy with a Hindu in religious ideas does not enable a man to become a Hindu. Admission of a man to the membership of the community is one thing, and converting a man to one's own belief is another thing. Conversion to religious ideas does not lead a man to the membership of the Hindu community.

As Hindu society is divided into a number of castes, membership of Hindu society cannot be obtained unless a man is admitted as a member of one of the castes. The castes do not suffer any control whatever by the Hindu community as a whole. The Hindu community is a federation, without central organization of any kind. So the whole Hindu community to-day cannot tell any particular caste whether any particular individual is eligible for admission into that caste. If any particular caste wishes to take in a foreigner, the Hindu community as a whole has no power to prevent it.

Again, there is another way by which a person, or a group of persons, can call themselves Hindus. All that is necessary is that that group of persons should begin to call itself Hindus. If they do that, nobody in the world can prevent it. Of course, almost all of the existing castes will decline to intermarry with the newly-formed group; but even the existing Hindu castes do not marry with each other. After a generation or two nobody would doubt their claim as Hindus. There has been a case where a Roman Catholic community, which quarrelled with their priests, and gave up Christianity, bought Hindu gods, worshipped them, and became Hindus. Nowadays, their claim to Hinduism is undisputed.

The question of the admission of foreigners into the fold has not been sufficiently brought forward, but the question of the "reclamation of the fallen," that is, readmitting those men who have given up Hinduism and have joined Christianity, or other ignoble (anārya) sampradāyas, has received considerable attention. Though attention has been brought to this question no rational methods have been adopted. At present this subject is one of those on which "social reformers" can display their zeal by eloquence, but how such a reclamation can be accomplished has hardly been understood by them.

The observation of facts solves the question in itself. If a man is converted to the Christian theophratry and wishes to return to Hinduism, all that he is anxious to do is give up his connexion with "the Christian caste" and enter his caste back again. In this case the proper authority to appeal to is the representatives of his own old caste. Appeal to the Hindu community in general or to Brāhmaṇas is useless. It is unnecessary first of all, and secondly, if it is done, it would not bring about the desired results. All that the Brāhmaṇas can do is to purify the individual, by giving him some kind of penance, but they cannot make him a member of any definite caste. The caste decides for itself as to who its members should be. If that caste or tribe is not organized; that is, if it has no central government, readmission of the fallen is difficult if not impossible. Brāhmaṇas have very often made experiments of giving purification to an individual, but such attempts have failed. That man becomes Hindu to be sure, nobody would question that part of the transformation, but he would not be able to find any people to make any connexion with him, or perhaps even to dine with him. He would thus become a member of "one-man caste" or would be compelled to make connexion with such people as would care to do that, very often with those who may have some kind of blemish already.

But, on the contrary, cases have happened where the fallen have been successfully reclaimed. Such has been the case specially in some of the lower castes which have a caste council. The council, or the general meeting convened by the council, would first decide whether a particular fallen man should be readmitted or not. When the caste has decided on taking the fallen in, then they call on the Brāhmaṇas to purify him, and such attempts have been successful.

These facts speak for themselves. The rule may be easily laid down as follows. Any caste may take the fallen, or foreigners, into their own body; and by being so included a person may become a full-fledged Hindu.

As the inclusion of a foreigner in the Hindu community is rendered extremely difficult by the Hindu caste system, so also is the case with exclusion of a Hindu by the Hindu community. Unless a person joins a non-Hindu caste like the Christian or the Mohamedan caste by accepting its "religions," that is, its social membership, a Hindu will not cease to be a Hindu.

In order to explain the fact mentioned above it is necessary to explain the exact nature of excommunication and its place in the Hindu social theory.

I have used the word excommunication in a sense wider than the one which is usually attached to it. I have used this word to express the ideas conveyed by the word "bahiṣhkāra" (bahis = outside, kāra = making or putting), which means cutting off the relations. This word includes the ideas conveyed by the words, excommunication (religions), ostracism, and boycotting.

As English and American readers may be ignorant of the "bahiṣhkāra," so also Indian readers are likely to be ignorant of the meaning of excommunication, as it is understood by the Western world. I first try to explain the terms. excommunication, ostracism and boycotting.

Excommunication

According to the Christian conception, excommunication is the highest ecclesiastical censure and the judicial exclusion of a baptized person from the fellowship of the visible Church of Christ. It is intended not so much to punish the culprit, as to correct him and bring him back to the path of righteousness. Excommunication is distinguished from the lesser punishments like suspension (for clerics) and interdicts. The excommunicated person does not, however, cease to be a Christian, since his baptism can never be effaced. Still, he is to be treated like an exile or a stranger by the community.

The textual authorities for excommunication are principally the following.

When Jesus asked the question of His disciples as to who He was, Simon Peter answered and said, "Thou art the Christ, the Son of the living God." And Jesus answered and said unto him, "Blessed art thou, Simon Bar-Jonah. . . . I will give unto thee the keys of the kingdom of heaven: and whatsoever thou shalt bind on earth shall be bound in heaven: and whatsoever thou shalt loose on earth shall be loosed in heaven" (Matt. xvi. 13–19).

"And if thy brother sin against thee, go, show him his fault, between thee and him alone. If he hear thee, thou hast gained thy brother, but if he hear *thee* not, take with thee one or two more, that at the mouth of two witnesses or three every word may be established. And if he refuse to hear them, tell it unto the Church: and if he refuse to hear the Church also, let him be unto thee as the Gentile and the publican" (Matt. xviii. 15–18).

Jesus said to His disciples after His resurrection: "Whosesoever sins ye forgive, they are forgiven unto them; whosesoever sins ye retain, they are retained" (John xx. 23).

In the first few centuries of the Christian era, excommunication was not supposed to be only cutting off of relations. It did not merely sever the bond which holds the individual to his place in the Church. The sentence pronounced on earth was supposed to be ratified in heaven. Hence Pope Leo X in the Bull "Exsurge Domine" (May 16, 1520) condemned Luther's twenty-third proposition, according to which "Excommunications are merely external punishments, nor do they deprive a man of the common spiritual prayers of the church."

Excommunication, in modern occidental society, has practically ceased to be effective. I have not heard of a single case in America where Protestants have formally excommunicated any persons, though expulsion from the church has been occasionally resorted to. But expulsion from the church of a person does not necessarily impose upon the other members of the church the duty of cutting off all relations with the expelled person, though many members may avoid him. In modern conditions, specially in America, a person excommunicated by the Roman Church is not likely to suffer or to feel any great social exclusion, because the excommunicated community, according to the Church of Rome, is very large. Persons who are Protestants are theoretically excommunicated. Freemasons are also considered as excommunicates. Again, in no country does excommunication impose any civil disability now.

Though excommunication has ceased to be effective, other measures which society has at its command are ostracism and boycott. By these society expresses its disapproval of certain actions and conditions, which the state does not care to recognize.

Ostracism

Ostracism at present means banishment from good society. It is, in fact, an unorganized excommunication.

Ostracism being unorganized, it differs in effect considerably from excommunication. Excommunication can be revoked at any time, ostracism cannot be revoked at any definite period.

Very often persons who are ostracized are gone for ever. Sometimes an ostracized person is taken back into society, when the society forgets or forgives the offence. As ostracism is unorganized, it is confined to a very small section of the society in ordinary cases, and becomes general only when the nature of the offence is grave. In America ostracism takes place in the following classes of cases.

The fact which can be very easily observed is that if a white man or woman marries a negro woman or man, the former is ostracized by the white race. Here the ostracism is all-pervading and spontaneous. There is no necessity for making the least effort to bring it about. All white people instinctively avoid the monster. The white individual goes out from the white caste and joins the caste of the negro.

Intermarriage between classes among Americans does cause some ostracism, but that ostracism is impermanent and is not very strong, one of the reasons being that the classes in America are not so strongly marked as they are in Europe.

There is still a great deal of ostracism, consequent upon the marriage with Jews. But even this ostracism is not very strong. Christian Americans will forsake the person who marries with Jews; and the Jews will do the same. But there is a section among both the peoples which tolerates and even approves of such marriages.

I think if any American becomes faithless to his country, the people in general will ostracize him, even though he may be forgiven by the government. Cases of this kind have been extremely few, but they have occurred.

Criminals are always ostracized by society, excepting in cases where a man is too rich to be excommunicated, or commits only a fashionable crime. Immoral women, or women who are seduced, are also entirely forsaken. The bastards, or illegitimate children, are generally ostracized, but such persons always move away from the districts where they are known and go somewhere else; and when they do so they can successfully conceal their status. It should be remembered here that in America it is not customary to inquire about a person's father or mother, as it is customary in the old world.

Boycotting

A boycott is a combination against a landlord, tradesman, employer or other person, whereby the persons enforcing the boycott cease social or business relations with the party boycotted, and seek to induce others to withhold having relations with him. It is used also of agreements not to use certain articles or the articles of a certain manufacturer. Boycotts, though largely conducted by trade unions, are by no means confined to them. Manufacturers boycott certain dealers, publishers boycott some booksellers, railroads boycott railroads, temperance people boycott certain persons, clergymen establish boycotts, even one nation boycotts another nation.

Bahiṣhkāra, or the system of excommunication, ostracism and boycotting, have become much less effective under the modern social conditions. Ostracism and boycotting exist and are considerably practised, but excommunication is not practised to any large extent. There are only a very few castes and some small localities where excommunication could be practised. In order to understand the reasons, therefore, it is necessary to learn some modern social conditions, and specially the influence of the West on Indian society.

CHAPTER VI

MODERN SOCIAL CONDITIONS

IN order to explain the system of bahiṣhkāra, as it operates on modern Hindu society, I feel compelled to introduce some details regarding the social conditions of the present day. I do this in order to accommodate my occidental readers, and I request Hindu readers not to be impatient at my introducing commonplace ideas and facts. It is likely that some occidental readers themselves may feel irritated at my giving a large space in this work to explain the social conditions, instead of theological and philosophical ideas which they may have been looking for. This disappointment of the Western readers would take place only because they have been previously misinformed that Hinduism is some kind of religion.

I shall confine myself principally to delineate the conditions in Mahārāshtra, or the Maratha country, as these conditions are more familiar to me than those of any other territory in India. I shall try to delineate the social composition in the Maratha country, and also the present disorganized state of the society, existing partly through inertia and partly through the clash of the Eastern and the Western traditions rendering social control and social reform difficult.

The Maratha country includes the greater part of the Bombay Presidency, Berar, a few districts in the Central Provinces and in the Nizam's domains. Marathas have also colonies in other parts of India, and specially in the states of Baroda, Indore, Gwaliar, Dewas, and Dhar, and also in the lapsed state of Tanjore.

The Maratha society is composed of various layers. First at the top there are Brāhmaṇas like Chittapāvana (Konkanastha), Deshastha and Karhādās, and Devarukhas. There are Sārasvatas and other Brāhmaṇas also in the Maratha country, but they have not yet been received by the Maratha Brāhmaṇas on terms of equality.

At the bottom of the society there are castes like Mahāra and Mānga. They are regarded as untouchables. This untouchable population includes about one-fourth of the people in the land.

Between these two extremes of social conditions are found castes likes Prabhus, Kunbi-Maratha, and the various trade castes like carpenter, goldsmith, coppersmith, barber, and others.

Among the intermediate castes, the caste of Kunbi-Marathas is the strongest. This caste is divided into two classes, Kunbis and Marathas, the latter being descendants of the families which came to the front during the days of the early Hindu kings in Dekhan, and those of the Mohamedans and Marathas. Shivaji, the founder of the Maratha empire, and the present Maratha princes belong to this caste. I speak of " Kunbi-Marathas " as one caste because the line between them is not sharp. At present this caste is almost entirely agricultural.

I should also add that, in the narrower sense, the Marathas are men of this Kunbi-Maratha caste, and in the larger sense all castes like Brāhmaṇas, Prabhus, and Mahāras are all Marathas. The Kunbi-Maratha caste forms one-third of the entire Maratha population.

The list of castes given herein is not complete. In fact, there are a large number of small castes which are not mentioned here, but the most important ones are given above.

The entire Maratha society is not a well-organized body. At present the society is without any central government whatsoever in social matters. The political government of the country is in the hands of the British, and consequently the Marathas are extremely anxious to prevent the strange race of rulers from interfering in their social matters, and the British Government also has refrained from making any social legislation. Even in cases when the Government was making a healthy law preventing the union of husband and wife before the female reaches the age of twelve, there was a strong opposition all over the country, not because the people disapproved of the measure itself, but because they denied to the Government the authority to undertake such legislation. The doctrine of *laissez-faire* has been thus carried in India to an extreme unknown in Europe on account of the separation, racial, religious, and social, between the rulers and people, and on account of the distrust caused thereby.

Thus the government is no controlling factor in the Maratha society, and all social matters are left to the people to be managed by themselves.

Unfortunately, the task which the British Government has now considered as lying outside their province the people have not been able to undertake, on account of the lack of any other organization which would be able to exact obedience. The progress of the people, therefore, to a certain extent, has been greatly retarded.

In order to appreciate fully the present conditions, it is necessary to review the sources of power in the Maratha community.

The Brāhmaṇas are still a power, but their power is extremely limited. All the power they have is that of advisers. They can tell what is proper and what is improper. They can tell which actions and conduct have scriptural sanction, and which have not, but they cannot compel any other caste to do anything. They again have a power of conferring Vedic or Puranic sacraments, as they are the priests of the nation, but the possibilities of this power, and the good uses to which this power can be applied, are not yet fully realized by them.

For example, if the Brāhmaṇas become a well-organized body, they can assume for themselves the power of conferring the Vedic sacraments on anybody they think fit, and the Maratha society would be perfectly willing to acquiesce in this assumption if they used this power for the benefit of the society. They can lay down rules for the other castes requiring them to attain a certain standard of education, compel them to observe certain moral rules in order to gain the benefit of the Vedic sacraments. The situation to-day is somewhat pitiful. The other castes demand of the individual Brāhmaṇas or the Brāhmaṇas of a certain locality the right of the sacraments. Thus the other castes thrust upon the Brāhmaṇas a power which, though it once belonged to the ancient Brāhmaṇas, the Brāhmaṇas of to-day are afraid to assume.

At present they follow this rule. All Brāhmaṇas have the right to Vedic sacraments, and no other people have any right to such sacrament. They appear to be willing to confer the Puranic sacraments on other higher castes in the country, to which shūdras are eligible.

The Brāhmaṇas themselves are not an organized body at present. Most of the Brāhmaṇas follow non-priestly occupations of various kinds, like those of physicians, lawyers, teachers and government servants. Those who follow the priestly occupations are not always versed in the Vedas, though they are well versed in the ritual that is connected with their profession. When any complicated question arises they guide themselves by the opinion of Shastrīs, i.e., those who are learned in Vedas, and Shāstras. In ordinary cities the number of such Shastrīs is limited. The Shastrīs in the ordinary cities generally give decision on questions that are brought before them, but in the cases of greater importance they generally guide themselves by the decisions of the body of scholars in places known for Sanskrit learning. In the Maratha country they are mainly the following: Poona, Nasik, Wai and Kolhapur. There is one authority greater than all these bodies of scholars. It is His Holiness, Shri Shankarāchārya of Sankeshvara. Many persons consider that the Sacred Seat of Shrigeri in Southern India is a still greater authority. But inasmuch as the "Man on the seat of Shṛingerī" stays outside Mahārāshtra, this authority is rarely appealed to, and even the Shankarāchārya of Sankeshvara is becoming more or less a nonentity.

The castes like Kunbi-Maratha are too large to control their members properly. In fact, a very large number of castes do not have any caste councils. For this reason many of the things which the central authorities in caste perform remain unperformed in the Maratha country.

Even the formal exclusion of a person is rarely done or even attempted. Thus excommunication is practically not resorted to. The function of formal excommunication has given place to ostracism. The nature of this ostracism can be best illustrated by describing the present condition of some caste.

Let us take the caste of Chittapāvana[1] (pure-hearted) or Konkanastha Brāhmaṇas to illustrate the matter. The home of this caste is Konkan, or rather the district of Ratnāgiri in Konkan. This caste is spread all over India, and holds at present leadership of the Maratha society.

Now if any member of the caste commits any infraction of the customs, say, eats meat, drinks liquor, or marries a widow, then in order to take action against him or even to exclude him from the community, it is necessary to have a council or some kind of government to pronounce a judgment. Some authority must pre-exist to take any action. At present there is none. In the days of the Peishwas the Peishwas themselves were such authority, not only for this caste but to a certain extent for all castes. Any question relating to religious observance or to social customs used to be discussed or decided in the court (durbar) of the Peishwas, or by the authorities of justice or by the college of Brāhmaṇas recognized by the Peishwas. The decision which would be given by the Peishwas' council in such matters would go undisputed from "Benares to Rameshvaram," i.e., all over India, and especially in the

[1] Some persons pronounce the word as *chit-pāvana*, and claim that the word means "purified by the funeral pile." There is a very interesting story regarding these Brāhmaṇas, explaining their origin from the corpses of fishermen, made alive by Parashurāma.

Maratha country. Even in English territory the opinion of the Peishwas in such matters would take effect, and was enforced by the British Government.

But the days of the Peishwas are gone, unfortunately, to return no more. At present there is no council, no definite authority to which appeal could be made and whose decision would be respected. Let us mark the effects.

The Peishwas are gone, and so is the power of the Shāstrīs and Pundits in Poona. The priests, Shāstris and Pundits in Poona still like to play their excommunication formalities. They often excommunicate persons, either those who have returned from England, or married a widow, or drank tea with Englishmen, but nobody pays attention to their excommunication excepting their own circle, which to-day has become very small and unimportant.

As in Poona, so in other places; the priests and Pundits of a town gather together to consider the case of a Brāhmaṇa culprit. Very often the culprit does not care to obey their summons, and the case is decided in his absence. The priests may pronounce an excommunication, but the culprit is not at all afraid of it, for their excommunication is not much regarded by the bulk, or at least by a considerable section of the Brāhmaṇa community. Very often the person excommunicated by the priests has far more influence in the society than that of all the priests in the town put together, and thus the excommunication by the assemblies of priests and Pundits have become a joke.

What is the reason of such a condition? Why is it that persons who are either the priests of the society, or men learned in Vedas and Shāstras, should not have enough influence on the society to cause at least ostracism of persons who have violated the traditional custom? The main reason is that the prestige of this class has disappeared with the spread of Western science and Western ideas. The Shāstrīs and Pundits are not the only representatives of learning. More than this: they are lacking in such learning as the society demands. The society finds it necessary to change; and the orthodox learning desires to stick to the old. The class of people who have greatest influence on the society to-day is the one which is oriented in the knowledge of Western as well as of Eastern lore. This class consists of men who are educated in colleges and schools where European sciences and philosophies, history, political economy as well as Sanskrit literature and philosophy are taught. This class has often produced Sanskrit scholars who would put the Shāstrīs and Pundits to shame, even in their own field. Again, this class controls the Press, and forms the public opinion.[1] A careful observer cannot also fail to notice the tendency, in recent years, on the part of certain newspapers in Poona towards the usurpation of that authority and prestige which once belonged to the assemblies of Pundits. These facts mean that the Pundits in India are not entirely the representatives or the formers of public opinion. They have a following, to be sure, but it is mostly among the classes less educated than the average, and among women.

Moreover, on account of the inevitable clash of the old and the new, of the Eastern and the Western, the population is divided into two classes: (1) The traditionalists (Uddhāraka), and (2) the reformers (sudhāraka). The

[1] The only important paper that is controlled by a man of orthodox education is *the Dharma* of Wai. The editor, a man of great learning, is known all over Mahārāshtra by his uncompromising attitude towards social reforms of various kinds.

division between them is not sharp, but one class imperceptibly merges into the other.

Shortly after the overthrow of the Marathas by the British in 1818, English education found its way into the Maratha country. Some classes of people on this account assimilated the English ideas, the English views of life, and with some people it became a fashion to imitate the English. These people called themselves and were called "reformers" (sudhāraka). This band consisted of men of several types. There were men who were tired of Brāhmaṇic ceremonial and of the strict discipline which Brāhmaṇism imposes, and wondered whether this ceremonial and discipline were necessary to attain eternal bliss. There were men who doubted the validity of Indian philosophy, and became agnostic towards the law of Karma, existence of God and transmigration of soul, and even about the existence of soul. There were men who considered English dress as superior to the Hindu dress, and also some among Brāhmaṇas who preferred animal food to vegetarian diet. There were men who disliked the old custom of early marriage, and of the prohibition of remarriage of widows. Some people imitated the English in their fashions as well as vices. Brāhmaṇas of this class began to drink liquor and eat animal food. One organ of this class, namely, the "Sudhāraka" of Poona, showed its "moral courage" by taking advertisements of liquor, a thing which no Maratha newspaper does! Men of the class mentioned last, by their misconduct, brought to a certain extent the whole sudhāraka band into disrepute.

The other class, the Uddhārakas (uplifters), or the traditionalists, regarded themselves as uplifters, or champions of the old. The tenets of this party, like those of the reformers, were never definite. There were, of course, men in society who regarded the present conditions as ideal and proper, provided the innovations introduced by the English-educated men could be eliminated. There were also men who held that whatever the ancient sages have said should be followed without any murmur. But besides such men there were a large number in this party who were lovers of order in the society and were not willing to divorce the old. Again, many of the reprehensible actions of the so-called "reformers" disgusted some people with the class of reformers—and these people swelled the ranks of Uddhārakas.

"Reformers" and "traditionalists" are not terms signifying any absolute tenets. A man who may be classed as a "reformer" in the village would not be classed as a "reformer" in a city. The chances are that he may be considered as a traditionalist by his urban neighbourhood. The same principle would hold good if we compared a small city to a large one. A native of Poona would do many things in Bombay which he would not dare do in Poona. A man who may be considered as a "reformer" in Poona will find himself lost if he goes to Bombay.[1]

The Maratha Brahmin community, and specially the Chittapāvana caste, has become extremely multiform in its ideas, and manners, and habits. On one hand, you may find among them men, who may be oriented in Western sciences, materialists in their ideas, imitating the Europeans in their dress and fashions, and in making use of animal food and liquors. On the other, you may find a man who

[1] Strangely enough, Amraoti, a small city of less than forty thousand population in Berar, has been considered as "the capital of the social reformers" in the Maratha country.

may regard himself and his caste as holiest of mortals, following all the orthodox Vedic rites, performing sandhyā three times a day, and spending over five hours in his sacerdotal practices. Both classes of men belong to the same caste, feel strong sympathy for each other notwithstanding all their differences, marry with each other with perfect freedom, and generally get along very well together, though their forefathers used to feel polluted by the food of a Sārasvata Brāhmaṇa, an important caste in the Maratha country, who differ from the Chittapāvana Brāhmaṇas only in the use of fish by the former in their diet, which the Chittapāvanas have prohibited to their own caste men.

Thus a man who belongs to the caste which represents priesthood may commit any infraction of the rules of convention or of scripture, or may do actions which even many non-priestly castes prohibit. He may engage himself in any trade he pleases. He may go and eat where he wants to, drink anything he desires, may go to a foreign country and act according to the manners of the foreign country, may refuse to make atonement for what a traditionalist Hindu regards as sin, and may still retain his position in the community, that is, may claim the membership of the sacred priestly caste, and his claim would go unchallenged. Even after doing all this, if he cares to take up the occupation of a priest, nobody would be able to prevent him from doing so.

Such is the latitude which men who belong to the Chittapāvana Brāhmaṇa caste can take. This would seem very ironical when we pay attention to the high claims and pretensions of this caste.[1]

[1] Maratha Brāhmins have unfortunately too great an opinion of themselves. They regard themselves not only as the élite of man-

But the above statement should not be construed as indicating that traditional ideals and principles are being surrendered by the bulk of the Brāhmaṇas, yet these ideals have become more reasonable. Most of the Brāhmaṇas observe the traditional principles of conduct and purity, and only feel sorry for the erring members of the community. Still they do not, I think, feel inclined to exclude the radicals or the erring men from the Brāhmaṇahood altogether. The ideas of purity and pollution have themselves become moderate.

This change in the ideas regarding purity and pollution has been brought about partly by the spread of occidental ideas, and partly by the changing economic conditions. The ideas of the Brāhmaṇas in this matter had become extremely extravagant since the Mohamedan conquest, reaching their zenith in the earlier part of the nineteenth century. Many rapid changes have taken place in this matter during the twenty years within the memory of the author. The psychic reason for these changes is simply this. Every man who has a certain ideal before him, or

kind because they are Brāhmins, but also because they regard themselves as superior to all other Brāhmins in India. To them Gujrath Brāhmins are only a caste of water-carriers, and Telang Brāhmins are a caste of cooks. They look upon Sārasvata Brāhmaṇas and the Brāhmaṇas of Northern India as degenerate because the latter are "fish-eaters." They again believe that all other Brāhmaṇas, like those of Northern India, have distorted tongues which renders them unfit to pronounce Sanskrit speech correctly. They again have a pride that they are the only Brāhmaṇas who resemble in any degree the Brāhmaṇas of ancient times; that is, that they are gifted with the wisdom required of a statesman and a scholar, and with the valour of a Kshatriya, to be used for the defence of the country when the country needs them to undertake the task. As a result of these sentiments of the Maratha Brāhmins they are far from popular, irrespective of the respect which they may inspire.

certain rules of conduct which he may wish to live up to, may sacrifice some of his pleasures and conveniences to those ideals and rules, but to this sacrifice there would be some limit. Should it become necessary to make a greater sacrifice in order to hold to the principle, some very few conscientious people may make the required greater sacrifice, but the bulk of the people would modify the principle in practice; but when the practice changes, it should not be understood that the rule is at once given up, though it tends to fall into disuse.

Now under the present conditions it has become impossible to maintain some of those rules of ceremonial purity, and an average man does not observe them.

For example: A Brāhmaṇa, or a high caste Hindu is supposed to take a bath if he touches a man belonging to one of the lowest castes (antyaja). This rule is fairly well observed in villages. In cities it is less observed. In large cities like Bombay, where it would be necessary to bathe a dozen times a day for the proper observance of the rule, it is dispensed with altogether.

Another example: Nowadays, many Hindus, including even the Brāhmaṇas in Bombay, have no scruples in eating in restaurants established by the Persians (Irans). Until the year 1894 there were no Hindu restaurants in Bombay. Unless a restaurant is conducted by a Brāhmana, Hindus of all castes will not eat in it. The Brāhmaṇas had not opened restaurants either because they shrank from the guilt of selling liquids (Skr. word is "rasa," which includes water, oil, or butter, or food cooked therewith); or because they did not realize the opportunity. The Brāhmaṇas who were working in the offices or other places used to feel the necessity of eating something at noon. Some persons who were very strict in maintaining the principle, took with them such eatables from home as could not be polluted by touch.[1] There were some who would satisfy their hunger by eating fruit. But there were also some who would not hesitate to resort to the non-Brāhmaṇical method of buying prepared food.[2] There were at this time tea-rooms and restaurants all over the town started by the Persians, where non-Hindus used to go and eat. These shops tempted the Brahmins and other Hindus to commit the irreligious act of eating prepared food without proper ceremonial, and that, too, from the hands of a Mlechchha. As a result of this, now, in Bombay it is an established custom for a Hindu to drink tea in an Irani restaurant. When Brāhmaṇas began to eat in an Irani restaurant they gave up gradually their scruples against eating other kinds of food

[1] There are some varieties of food which would be very easily polluted, e g., bread made in water. Such a bread a man cannot eat at any time. He should eat it only after bathing and wearing a specially consecrated cloth. The bread also must be specially prepared with such ceremonial purity. If any bread is to be left over for another meal, it should be kept in a select and ceremonially pure place in the house by a man who may be in the pure condition described above. Bread made in milk does not demand so many formalities in order to guard against pollution. You can make the bread in milk, put it in a can of tinned brass, put it in your pocket, and may go to another place, even wearing a shoe made of cow-hide; but still the bread could not be polluted. Articles like Peḍha, which are made of milk and sugar only, would not be polluted even if a Mohamedan, Christian, or a low caste Hindu touched them. Fruit cannot be polluted at all, as long as it is physically pure. Nowadays, with the growing scarcity of milk in large cities, Brāhmins have to remain satisfied with bread made in water, and have to concede to such bread the privileges of the bread made in milk.

[2] Eating cooked food is an act which should be performed with due regard to ceremonial; and such ceremonial cannot be observed in a market place. Hence there is an objection to buy prepared food.

prohibited to a Brāhmaṇa, which are available in a Persian restaurant. Such a place is very well suited for the purpose of eating improper food because Hindus, like other peoples, generally trust a foreigner more, in things of which they make a secret, or upon which society frowns.

The influences which brought about a moderation in the feelings of purity and pollution are many; the principal ones may be summarized as follows. First, with the growth of industrial institutions and in the changes in the social structure and institutions caused thereby, it became impracticable to maintain the old rules of purity and pollution in their entirety without any serious inconvenience in life. Second, when the changes in the old customs became necessary, the European ideas and philosophy which are now studied by Indians, justified the rationality of what according to old ideas was considered improper and impure. The younger generation began to appeal to the principles of physical purity and impurity instead of the old ideas of ceremonial purity and impurity which the old shāstras (sciences) inculcated. Third, the system of Western medicine, which made its way into the country, compelled people to take up and consume those things which they regarded as impure, e.g. brandy, cod-liver oil, etc. Fourth, increase of skill, or rather the European skill, presented the "impure" substances in a less disagreeable form, and when they are so presented to the people they do not hurt the sensibilities of the people. For example, if you present to a Marātha Brāhmaṇa a cod-fish and ask him to eat it he would not do so, but if you give him cod-liver oil he would have less objection to take it. No Brāhmaṇa would, for example, eat any fat of the cow, but if you give him a piece of pie, his sensibilities would not be hurt while eating it. An orthodox Brāhmaṇa would not like to drink water from the hands of a shūdra, but when it comes through a pipe he has no objection to drink it, though theoretically it should cause just as much pollution, because many low castes, even impure Englishmen, may be working on the reservoir of water which gives water to a Brāhmaṇa.

When a society becomes habituated to the use of an "impure" article in a disguised form, it becomes slowly willing to use "impure" articles in a less disguised shape. If many Brāhmaṇas become used to cod-liver oil, then some of them may feel no scruples against eating fish itself. This fall from the standard of purity has another very valuable psychological effect. The abhorrence which a man feels towards other people decreases. An orthodox Brāhmaṇa, I should say most of the Brāhmaṇas to-day, feel that they are superior to the rest of the Hindus, as their bodies are pure, while those of the rest of the Hindus are more or less impure. Hindus in general regard themselves as purer than the rest of the world. One of the most important reasons why Hindus, and among them Brāhmaṇas, regard themselves as purer and more sacred than the rest, is that they are more particular as to what they eat. Thus a fall from the Brāhmaṇical ideals of purity, and even a fall from the ideals of morality, tends to make the people more democratic. It does not mean that a Brāhmaṇa who uses animal food begins to look upon a lower caste man as his equal, but the abhorrence for him becomes much less. Very often we observe men who have occasionally erred, and have left the right path; when they become reclaimed they have a great deal of sympathy for their erring fellow-men, because they realize better that a man who errs is not altogether a bad man, that they have done themselves what people condemn, and that they have been often treated unjustly by their brothers for a slight deviation from the approved path. On the contrary, those who are stern in their adherence to moral principles became rather too severe towards their fellow-men. Similar is the case with the Hindus. If a Brāhmaṇa eats animal food occasionally, then his abhorrence of those people who have a custom of eating such food becomes less. For this reason, a temporary use of the animal food, and even of liquor, by the Brāhmaṇas should not cause us much pain. I think if the Brāhmaṇas becomes less puritanic in their ideas and conduct, notwithstanding a temporary loss it may cause to the morals of the society, the latter will be an ultimate gainer rather than a loser.

Perhaps it may interest the Western reader to know how the changed conditions operate on the Hindu mind and prepares it to accept changes in their manners and customs.

The changes in the customs of the Hindus are brought about by the environments; and European ideas and philosophy give them only arguments to justify their conduct or to silence their scruples. But even the European philosophy does not always suffice to answer the dictates of conscience (the moral attitude which may have become reflex). European philosophy is freely taken over by the Hindus to understand the nature of things; but it is much less often borrowed as a guide to conduct, excepting in cases where Hindus themselves have very little in the way of positive ideas and customs on those subjects. Thus dealing with commercial and legal matters the Hindus try to find out the European customs and the English law on the subject. Very often they borrow European notions, regarding "good manners." But there are some things which they do not freely borrow. It is especially the case when they have some rules already on those matters to which they adhere. In Europe or America, if the people simply know the Hindu or the Chinese ideas, regarding the propriety and impropriety, very little change in the occidental customs will be brought about, even if they see the rationality of the ideas of the Orientals. Similar is the case in India. If the Hindus believe in the rationality of some European ideas, but have too great a regard for their own traditions to discard them, the changes in the traditional customs take place by the introduction of fictions. Let me give a few concrete cases to illustrate the process, where the people tried to make the rules of purity and pollution suitable to modern times.

(1) Rules of purity and pollution require that a high caste man should not drink water touched by a low caste man; if he does drink he should make an atonement. When the water was supplied to individual families in the cities by the pipes, the question arose whether a man becomes polluted by drinking that water, and if so is it necessary for him to make an atonement. When this question came before the council of a certain caste, they declared that the water tax which the people pay for using the water to the city or to the government may be regarded as an adequate fine to make that atonement.

(2) When many Hindus received treatment from European physicians, the medicine which the physicians gave often contained water. Now water touched by a European is impure. Sometimes the medicine which the physicians gave contained even brandy. The propriety of drinking that medicine began to trouble the Hindu

conscience. A Sanskrit text came to their aid in the difficulty. It says "Medicine (whatever it may be) is (as sacred as) the water of the Ganges, and the physician (should be respected) like the (God) Nārāyana, the remover (of pain or sin)."

(3) When many Hindus began to drink tea in the restaurants of the Persians, they began to justify their conduct by declaring that the Persians are more or less Hindus, and that their forefathers were the brothers of Hindus.

(4) For a certain number of purposes it is necessary to use the water of the Ganges, which has a purifying power, to clear some kinds of pollution. In distant parts of India many people keep some water from the Ganges for special occasions. The water is generally scarce, and the uses to which it could be put are many. Again, if one family has any quantity of it, say, about a pint or a quart, all the families in the neighbourhood would like to have some use of it in the case of extreme necessity. Then in order to make the water go for a long time the following method is resorted to. One or two drops of the Ganges water is poured in a gallon of ordinary water. Thus that gallon is converted into Ganges water. This procedure is justified on the ground that when a stream flows into the river Ganges the water of the stream is converted into water of the Ganges.

All this procedure may seem ludicrous; but if properly considered there is nothing bad or blameworthy about it; if we have laws, certain rules of conduct, they generally leave a strong impression on our minds. If we wish to deviate from the established moral principle very few of us can satisfy our conscience or justify ourselves in the eyes of the world around us by the principle of expediency only. We generally try to seek some other moral backing. If any man wishes to do anything that he thinks to be morally unjustifiable, and if he finds with the help of an expert lawyer that his conduct is perfectly legal, then he becomes greatly nerved. He knows that some sort of philosophy or law justifies his actions. As with law, so with scriptural injunction or traditional rule; scriptural permission to do anything, or some justification by orthodox principle, adds a great deal of strength.

This process is not modern. It is not peculiarly Indian. Let me give an example. In the eighteenth century one of the Peishwas of Poona had accepted an invitation to dine at the house of a Brāhmaṇa nobleman on a certain day. But in the meanwhile the nephew of the nobleman died in battle; and for this reason the nobleman was under impurity for ten days, and the day of the invitation fell within those ten days, Now, it is not proper for anybody to receive food in the house of a mourner during those ten days. The chief secretary of the Peishwa was unwilling to offend the nobleman, by advising his master not to dine with him. He consulted a Brāhmaṇa shāstri (a scholar, a scientist), as to whether the dharma shāstra can find any authority to permit eating in the house of that nobleman. The Bráhmaṇa discovered a Sanskrit text, which said that, "Those who die for the nation are not dead." Thus the nephew of the nobleman is not dead, and so that nobleman is not a mourner.[1]

The aim of introducing all these details regarding the social conditions of the Maratha country is to explain

[1] I do not guarantee the truth of the story, but it seems probable to me. I do not even remember whether I have heard of this story or read it.

how excommunication, ostracism, and boycotting are practised in the Maratha country; and for this purpose it may be well to recapitulate what I have just said. In the Maratha country there is no organization controlling all the castes of Hindu society except the British Government, and the British Government does not exert any influence in social matters. The Brāhmaṇas are still a power, but inasmuch as their caste is unorganized they are not able to exert it in a useful manner. The colleges of Shastrīs and Pundits, which have still kept up the habit of pronouncing bahiṣhkāra, have become powerless, mainly for three reasons. First, in order to secure the confidence and the respect of the people, and to get their decisions obeyed by the people, they ought to have a power delegated by the government or by the people; but this is not the case. Secondly, there is a class of educated Brāhmaṇas in society which is not entirely in sympathy with the ideas of the Shastrīs, and Pundits, and which to-day has more prestige in society than the old-fashioned Pundits. And thirdly, society itself is in a process of transformation as regards ideas, principles and customs. It is divided into parties, one party approving and the other party disapproving the departures from the traditional rules.

In such a condition of affairs, exclusion of a man by the entire Hindu community by a formal excommunication is impossible.

Formal excommunication of a man by his caste is also impossible if the caste is not well organized.

Though excommunication has to a great extent disappeared, still ostracism continues to exist. Boycotting is often practised. Even excommunication is also practised to a small extent.

Excommunication by a Village

The cases in which a number of castes or men belonging to different castes join together to excommunicate a man and to make his condition wretched necessarily occur within a very small area, i.e. in a village. When a whole village excommunicates an individual, the people in the village would refuse him any kind of mutual help, and would refuse him service as well as patronage. In former times one of the principal things which were denied to such a person was fire, but nowadays with the introduction of lucifer matches the force of this measure is not available. These excommunicated persons may not get the Brāhmaṇas in the village to perform sacerdotal functions in their homes. They may not get even barbers to shave them, or washerman to wash their clothes, or even a cobbler to mend their shoes. Sometimes even the village shopkeeper is warned to refuse to sell them anything.

This social or complete excommunication is possible only in small places. In cities it is not possible to enforce any such excommunication, as people do not gather together easily to pronounce any judgment. On this account, and for many other reasons, manners in the cities are more lax.

This system of village excommunication takes notice not only of "religious" offences, but also of some other misdeeds, entirely unconnected with worship, ritual or ceremonial and social observances. I have known cases wherein some families were excommunicated by the villagers simply because those families did not pay their debts to another person in the village. Again, this system of excommunication is directed to control not only the so-called Hindus, but also non-Hindus. I have noticed that in certain villages the Maratha Jews have refrained from killing the cow for fear of being excommunicated by the villagers. The only things which the Jews are afraid of in an Indian village are the refusal of service by the barber, washerman, shopkeeper, physician, and above all the loss of patronage. The refusal of the Brāhmaṇas to do any service cannot have effect in the case of a Jew.

In the case of a Hindu, as I have said, there is no likelihood of his being excommunicated from the entire Hindu society, as the entire Hindu society is not organized. Members of some castes which have a central council have to fear excommunication from the caste, but this does not mean excommunication from the whole Hindu community. Members of castes which are not organized have no fear of expulsion from the caste, though in cases where they do actions which strikes the whole caste with horror, the resultant ostracism would practically amount to an excommunication.

Excommunication by the Caste

The castes which have a very strong central council are mostly the tribes which are recently Hinduized and have retained their traditional chiefs. In the Maratha country only a few trade castes have councils. The majority of the population, over seventy per cent. of people, are members of castes which do not have any central council. The part of India where almost all castes are strongly organized is, I think, Gujerath. In this province the cases of excommunications from castes are many and frequent.

When a man is expelled from his caste, it should not be understood that all Hindus begin to look upon him with horror. Very often the expulsion from caste of an individual or family is caused by a personal dislike. Almost all Hindus but those of his caste would treat the man just as they did before. The majority of Hindus would look upon that man as being as much a full-fledged Hindu as any other member of his caste. Again, almost always the individual is taken back into the caste on the receipt of a fine which the caste prescribes. Very often a large number of individuals are expelled from the caste on account of certain offences. This expulsion very often produces a caste, which the old caste looks down upon. When a person is excommunicated he really belongs to no caste, and therefore his condition becomes wretched. The people of his caste would form no matrimonial alliance with him, would not even dine with him. It should also be remembered that a man prior to his exclusion by the caste could contract marriages with his own class.

The only thing by which a man ceases to be a Hindu is the formal alliance with Christianity or Mohamedanism. This is primarily due to the fact that Christians and Mohamedans do not call themselves Hindus, and apply the term Hindu to those Indians who are neither Christians nor Mohamedans nor Parsees nor Jews. According to the Hindu theory, when a man becomes a Christian all that takes place is that he gives up his own caste and joins the caste of Christians.

Boycotting is considerably practised all over India. One caste very often boycotts another caste ; that is, refuses to do them habitual service. Suppose some quarrels arise between some barbers and some carpenters ; then the barber caste in order to punish the carpenters would refuse them service and thus bring them to terms. Boycotting does not always help a caste to get the desired result, however. The success of a caste depends on their indispensibility. For example, a butcher cannot possibly boycott a Brāhmaṇa, for a Brāhmin has no use for meat. The castes or trades that can succeed in boycotting are, barbers, washermen, scavengers and priests. The first three can boycott easily, because a Hindu of respectability thinks it degrading to take to any of these three occupations; and a priest can boycott, because no other people but Brāhmaṇas are allowed to become priests. When the colleges of priests pronounce a bahiṣhkāra on a non-Brāhmaṇa, it should not be construed as an excommunication. It is merely a priestly boycott; though cases happen when a few non-Brāhmaṇa families which are boycotted by the priests are excommunicated or ostracised by their own caste, and thus the priestly boycott has often an appearance of excommunication.

The aim of giving so many pages to the problem of *bahiṣhkāra*, is to explain its entirely social and not religious character. Bahiṣhkāra is never practised as far as theological or philosophical opinion is concerned. It is practised only for the violation of the rules of conduct. The reason why baptism of a Hindu causes excommunication from his caste and from Hinduism is not the belief, but his membership of a caste which does not claim membership of Hinduism.

CHAPTER VII

ORTHODOXY AND HETERODOXY

THE preceding chapter, which gives the modern social conditions, dwells also on the process of transformation of the Hindu society. In order to understand the exact nature of this transformation as contrasted with the previous attempts towards "social reform" made by the men of the type of Gautama and Basava, it is necessary to draw distinction between orthodoxy and heterodoxy.

The words "orthodoxy" and "heterodoxy" are likely to cause some surprise to the reader. He will say that almost every form of thought has its place in the Hindu treatment of knowledge and action (Jñāna and Karma). When the freest discussion has been tolerated in the Brāhmaṇa circle, what place can there be for orthodoxy and heterodoxy?

In fact, a distinction of this kind is of very late growth. And the distinction does not concern itself with any forms of thought, but concerns itself only with such actions as affect the social structure. There are nowadays plenty of reformers in India arising in every corner, and on account of the actions of these reformers some distinctions have come into existence.

The present social structure is capable of reform in two different manners. For the sake of convenience we may denominate these methods: orthodox (paramparā-sammata) and heterodox (paramparā-patita).

It is necessary here to explain the meaning of the two terms used above. The Sanskrit terms given in the brackets are to-day used in conversation and occasionally in newspapers by Maratha Brāhmins, and this distinction is differentiated from the distinction between sudhāraka and uddhārakas, that is, between reformers and traditionalists, on whom I have dwelt in the preceding pages.

Orthodoxy should never be confounded with conservatism of manners, customs and ideas. A heterodox (paramparā-patita) may be conservative of old ideas, while a radical reformer, even a hater of everything old, may also be orthodox. The meaning of these two words will become clear by concrete historical illustrations.

A Jain or a Lingavat holding very closely to the old ideas, which may be very similar to the ideas of an orthodox traditionalist, may still be regarded as a follower of heterodoxy, while a Brāhmin forsaking the old ideas but not joining a new sampradāya with a separate social existence will not be regarded as heterodox. He will still remain a member of the orthodox community. If he becomes a Brahmo he will not be regarded as belonging to the orthodox (paramparā-yukta, and not uddhāraka) community.

During the long period of thought and the social changes in India, there have been many sampradāyas which have been regarded as orthodox, and some others were regarded as heterodox. The former, which paid heed to the traditional principles of the social system, were orthodox. These appeared and disappeared, and happily so. As an important sampradāya of this character I may name the Bhāgwatas. But there were also others who disregarded the traditional principles and were, therefore, regarded as heterodox. These heterodoxies or the disturbing elements of society also have been many, and among them I may name Jainism, Buddhism, Mahānubhāvas, Lingavats, the Swāmi Nārāyanas, the Brahmos and several others. There has been very little in the theological opinions or philosophy of these sampradāyas, to which orthodoxy would have a strong objection; in fact, most of the ideas which these heterodox bodies have put forth have been held by many orthodox sampradāyas. But there has been one thing which orthodox Hinduism did not tolerate, and it is the formation of new tribes with a separate social existence with some theological doctrine wise or stupid at the basis.

Some heterodoxies have their origin in the rejection of the Brāhmaṇical sacrament and ritual and by the adoption of new ones. This has been, in fact, the most prominent cause of heterodoxy, that is, of the social separation of a sampradāya from the general population. In fact, no cult, no theological doctrine, is sufficient by itself to sever the individual from his tribe and to make him a member of a new tribe unless new ceremonies are instituted, which come into conflict with the old. In fact, orthodoxy can be defined as a regard for ancient Brāhmaṇical sacraments and heterodoxy as systematic neglect thereof as a matter of principle. It is not even necessary to observe all the sacraments, but it is specially necessary to observe the sacrament of initiation, which gives an individual born in an Ārya family the twice-born status. Buddhism, Jainism, Mahānubhāvism, Brahmoism are all heterodoxies, and for this reason primarily. The Prarthanā-samāja of Bombay is not, I think, heterodoxy because their members do not neglect the rituals. If any new sampradāya should rise, which should despise the Brāhmaṇical rites of marriage and try to substitute a civil marriage, and if the members of that body should be well organized, then that sampradāya is likely to become a heterodoxy.

It may be argued that if the members of the sampradāya became separated from the general society around them, then it is not the fault of the sampradāya, but it is the fault of the society. But this argument is not sufficiently cogent. It is the duty of the founders and the followers of the new sampradāyas, of the introducers of social innovations and advocates of foreign religions to understand the nature of the society they have to deal with. In case they do not take pains to understand the nature of the society when they take a jump, and find themselves paid for the innovation by social exclusion, they must bear it without any murmur. Cursing the society around them, when there is nobody to bear the blame, as the society is unorganized, is the work of cowards, who deserve pity indeed, but not sympathy. This opinion of mine I express with special reference to the high-caste Hindus who become Christians, and to the men who talk against caste, organize a religious brotherhood or tribe of their own to "abolish caste," start new sacraments, trample the old ones, find themselves excluded from the society, and therefore complain again. Had the whole society been well organized with a central head which could do or undo things, then only would their censure of the society have been of avail; but as long as that condition does not exist, to censure "society" or even the caste system is only worthy of the ignorant. But I am sorry to say that in such an attempt are found people of all classes—from a schoolgirl of ten years to the Hindu judges of the high court.

It is a fate of the heterodoxies or religions to become new castes, and thus a great source of annoyance. If a heterodoxy should succeed in absorbing the various tribes in a locality, it would create a nation separated from its fellow-men by worship, code of morals, scriptures, and in fact everything in life. The success of such a heterodoxy in India would ultimately create a conflict similar to that between Mohamedans and Christians along the Mediterranean Sea. The ultimatum of the heterodoxies is not a very happy one.

Let us now understand the principles of orthodoxy and see how they determine the principles of social reform.

The working principle of orthodoxy is to make numerous small changes as the time may require ; and to make these changes in such a manner that the innovators may not become a tribe of out-castes. If any number of thinkers hold any theological or philosophical doctrine, there would be no opposition from society, for the question of doctrine concerns only the philosophers, and the general public is indifferent as to that question. If they wish to make any changes in the social customs, they would introduce changes, taking care that they remain members of the society ; it is true that if the change is not very great, then the conservatives, though they may frown on them, will not attempt, or will not succeed in the attempt, to frustrate them. Another method of theirs is to keep the two questions, namely, that of social reform and theological creed, distinct. The reformers (sudhārakas) in the Maratha country who have not joined the heterodox bodies like the Brahma-samāja may be given as example of this class. These men are not willing to abolish the old rites or forms of worship, but have concentrated their attention on pure questions of social reform. The methods of these reformers (sudhārakas)are perfectly orthodox (parampara-sammata).

Orthodoxy has not yet formally laid down the principles of remodelling the society. The author himself thinks that it is possible to reconstruct society following the orthodox principles. Explanation of those methods involves a programme too long to be included in this volume; still some broad principles of social evolution which, if properly understood and applied for the purpose of social reform, will accelerate the remodelling of the society, deserve enunciation. I should also add that an application of those principles will perfectly be in conformity with the orthodox practice.

CHAPTER VIII

THEORY OF SOCIAL EVOLUTION

A PERUSAL of the preceding discussion will give the readers some facts regarding the formation of Hinduism and also tendencies which will determine its future. It may do more. It may give the theory of social evolution as reflected in the history of one-sixth of the human race. For the convenience of the reader I recapitulate here the theoretical position from the preceding chapters with some additions.

There have been some theories regarding social evolution already put forth by many writers. Unfortunately many of those theories have been products of imagination unaided by sound historical research.

The words "social evolution" have been used in the meaning of the general progress of mankind. The special phase of the social evolution paid attention to here is the history of the formations of social groups.

The process which has taken place in the world may be summarized as follows.

Since the descent of man from the lower species human beings are migrating all over the world in search of maintenance. They migrate in tribes. Some people from these tribes separate from their brothers, and develop new tribes and new peculiarities, physical and cultural.

There is thus a long period in human history of separation and differentiation.

After some greater development of civilization there comes a period of communication, association and intermixture.

Larger social groups are formed by absorption of the smaller. The elements which bring about this phenomenon are political conquest, creation of common culture by contact, and absorption of tribes by some religions.

Spread of religions and the spread or creation of a common civilization are important factors which lead to the unification of tribes and peoples. The influence of the spread of religions has been great in creating the Christian and the Mohamedan worlds. The history of Hinduism, of China, and of Japan shows the working of the other process. This process has done a great deal of work prior to the rise of the two Semitic theophratries. In India the religions or theophratries also tried to do the same work, but have not yet succeeded. The religions have succeeded in unifying tribes and peoples, but they have sowed deep the elements of disunion also. It has been the spirit of disunion and separatism that has promoted the unity among the co-religionists. I have stated in the preceding chapters the work of the process of religions (theophratries) and also of the *process of contact*.

The word "religion" being peculiarly a modern occidental word, I have tried to form a definition thereof at the beginning of this work by making a direct observation of the popular ideas among the Western peoples. I have also shown that a definition formed in this manner is useful in the study of the occidental phenomena only. As the phenomena denoted by the word religion do not exist in other countries, and in other civilizations, the word "religion" has no equivalents in other languages. One essential characteristic of a "religion" is that it is the tradition of a theophratry, that is, tribe or brotherhood based on theological doctrine or worship.

I have then examined the Hindu system by itself, and have shown, that according to Hindu terminology the word which comes nearest to the word "religion" is *sampradāya*. I have regarded this word as one of scientific value, and to convey its meaning I have used the word *theophratry*.

For the purposes of sociology two kinds of tribes should be distinguished. They are (1) socio-political (natural) tribes, and (2) theophratries (tribes based on theological doctrine or worship).

Theophratries are necessarily later growths. They can arise only when the protection of the individuals in the theophratry is guaranteed by an existing political society.

Theophratries, by the institution of new gods, methods of worship, sacraments, customs, ceremonies, feast days and holidays, give rise to dissimilarities, and thus create a division in the tribe or nation. Thus theophratries are anti-social in their very nature. The theophratries are always a nuisance to a nation unless the theophratry is co-extensive with the nation, that is, all the members of the nation are members of the theophratry.

If all the members of a nation are also members of the theophratry, and if that theophratry is doing missionary work, then the theophratry and the nation become a nuisance to the neighbouring nations; a portion of a neighbouring nation becomes like the missionary nation, and unlike the other members of their own nation. It becomes more sympathetic to foreigners, and less sympathetic with the people of their own nation.

Again, theophratries are a great hindrance to progress, specially as far as the rise of new ideas regarding God and morals are concerned. In tribes, notwithstanding its tribal worship and traditions, thought is more free. For in the latter case the unity of the group can exist without insistence on any particular doctrines. While in the theophratries some particular ideas, practices and doctrines stand at the very foundation of society; and to depart from them is regarded by the members of the theophratry as heretical and anti-social. This particular unfortunate situation leads to persecutions unworthy of any civilized people.

For the welfare of humanity it is desirable that these theophratries should either disappear or loosen their hold on men. The idea of the formation of a social group on the basis of worship or theological doctrine, instead of basing it on geographical and on political lines, is absurd in itself. These theophratries should not therefore be allowed to dabble with the existing social structure. The theophratrics may be formed and continued as long as they confine themselves to worship only, but they should be prevented from going beyond their sphere.

The sentiments which are expected to govern the life of a Hindu strongly are not sentiments regarding the theophratry, or moral ideas claiming particular allegiance to a theophratry, but dharma, or the ideas of duty, irrespective of the mandates of a theophratry. I have shown that the Hindus do not regard Christianity as a dharma. They regard it only as a sampradāya.

The main distinction between a religion and the tradition of a tribe is that religion is a self-defined thing, and the followers are supposed to follow the religion as it is. In the case of a tribal tradition, the tribe is a self-defined object, and the tribal tradition is variable. It is what the tribe will make. The sampradāyas in course of time may become tribal traditions, in case the sampradāya restricts the membership and allows the ideas and traditions to change freely and openly. If they do so they cease to be sampradāyas or religions. On the other hand, if a tribe opens its doors to other people on their acceptance of the tradition of the theological doctrines and the worship of the tribe, then the tribe becomes a religion or theophratry.

A sampradāya or theophratry expands and produces a common culture among a large number of heterogeneous tribes. But that process is materially different from the process which led to the formation of Hinduism. In one case the different tribes are made to accept uniform ideas by a conscious effort, and the admission of the foreign individuals to the theophratry is made expressly on that condition. In the other case the unity of ideas, thoughts, and manners results from the intercourse, spread of literature, arts, etc., from a tribe which may have superiority in this matter over the sister-tribes.

The Christian world and the Mohamedan world are thus creations of the sampradāya method, and Hinduism is the creation of the other process.

Theophratries have some advantages over the unification brought by the *process of contact* which is a characteristic of Hinduism. They try to abolish uncompromisingly indigenous civilizations of the tribes, calling them Heathenism; and thus the amount of uniformity which they are able to produce is greater. Again, within the theophratry there is less distinction of race or tribe, because the formation of a new tribe is aimed at, and therefore there is some appearance of equality. Again, the basis of the unification is simple. All that is required is a common worship and common theological doctrine.

The working of the *process of contact* which led to the formation of Hinduism, has some advantages as well as disadvantages. The latter are mainly these. There is no inducement to adopt the doctrine of the equality of tribes. As the formation of a new tribe is not aimed at, the old tribal distinctions are preserved. As the various original differences do exist, the tribes remain separate as they were before, and as a natural result they often become grouped in a hierarchy. These various tribes which are brought together are not bound together by all-pervading strong ties. To unite them strongly into one group and to promote greater uniformity some other feelings are necessary.

In India there was no feeling of Hindu unity until the foreign theophratrics of Mahomet and Christ made their appearance. This feeling of uniformity is created by contrast—contrast in the theological doctrines, gods, dress, manners and customs.

India is at present a battle-ground of religions and other theophratries. Each theophratry is trying its best to gain converts. But it is not likely that any of these will succeed in absorbing the entire population. The chances for a new theophratry are still less. Any attempt to unite India by the process of theophratry means promotion of mutual hatred and the postponement of Indian unity.

The feeling for theophratry is not only injurious to

India, but it is injurious to the world. The tendency of the modern world is not to allow the theological doctrine to become formative of the social group, but to create a feeling of brotherhood irrespective of the membership of theophratry. The defeat of the theophratries is bound to take place in two ways. The Church, which is the instrument for the promotion of the feeling for the theophratry, will either be forsaken or be reformed. People will not join the Church, and the class of actions of men which the Church used to control is becoming less. Moreover, the tradition common to the world at large independent of the theophratries will be so great that the traditions of a particular church, religion, or theophratry will be but a small portion, which would be regarded as negligible in social relations.

The two processes which lead to the uniformity of civilization among peoples have been discussed. They form part of the integration of world society. Social integration is in fact doing its work at every stage of a social group. Integration is taking place in all organisms, whether biological or social. Herbert Spencer has noticed several peculiarities of social organisms. He says:—

Societies agree with individual organisms in four conspicuous peculiarities:—

1. That commencing as small aggregations, they insensibly augment in mass: some of them eventually reaching ten thousand times what they originally were.
2. That while at first so simple in structure as to be regarded as structureless, they assume in the course of their growth a continually increasing complexity of structure.

3. That though in their early undeveloped states there exists in them scarcely any mutual dependence of parts, their parts gradually acquire a mutual dependence, which becomes at last so great that the activity and life of each part is made possible only by the activity and life of the rest.
4. That the life of a society is independent of, and far more prolonged than, the lives of any of its component units, who are severally born, grow, work and reproduce and die, while the body politic composed of them survives generation after generation, increasing in mass, in completeness of structure, and in functional activity.

It is the third peculiarity which deserves special attention here. It is in fact the core of social integration which deserves a thorough treatment.

When a large number of small social groups are put together to form a large uniform social group, then the resultant process which brings about the rearrangement of the molecules of society with the object of creating new structure is called *integration.* The tribes which come together and form large groups do not always succeed in the effort. In order to free the individual by shattering the tribal chains, and enclose him in the circle of the nation, it takes a great deal of effort. The federation of tribes before it reaches the final stage of a large tribe or a nation has to pass through a series of steps; and these steps may be easily discovered if one surveys the peoples in the world. Those steps are illustrated in caste systems, empires and hereditary classes, which may be given as examples of societies where the social integration has not been completed.

Caste system is an inevitable condition of a society in which there are a number of endogamous tribes occupying the same territory, and which tribes as a natural result of their endogamy become grouped in a hierarchy.

When many tribes are subordinated to one political power, and where the political power does not reduce the various tribes, speaking many languages and following various religions, to the condition of a social unit, then the society so constructed may be called an empire.

Sometimes the ruling tribe in an empire becomes less exclusive, then the ruling tribe may become a hereditary class.

But when the various tribes are reduced to a uniformity and become one tribe, then they may be considered as a perfectly integrated body.

In biology the term integration is applied to a process by which the manifold is compacted into relatively simple and permanent? In sociology the word may be used in the same sense. This term does not in fact belong to any particular science; but to the evolutionary philosophy in general. In social development the function of integration means simply the creation of one uniform tribe out of the federation of several tribes. Various tribes may have various languages, cultures, habits and manners, and to integrate them means to unify them. This integration is aided by a number of factors.

Political conquests and federations, propaganda of religions, development of a larger social consciousness, production of a similarity of civilization by intercourse, intermarriage between races and classes, unified language, economic adjustment among tribes, races and nations—all these promote social integration. It is impossible to enumerate these aids to integration in their totality. It is also equally difficult to explain the working of each of the above-mentioned aids, but explanation of one or two may be indulged in.

The factors of social integration are the following. First of all there should be groups of men to be integrated and to form new social groups. Secondly, there should be some reasons or aids to integration. There should be some definite reason why the two or more societies originally distinct should give up their isolated distinctiveness and form one society. Generally such integration of two or more societies into one society is gradual and very often unwilling. Generally political conquest, or political union against a common foe, lays the foundation for the formation of larger social groups. Missionary religions and civilizations often perform the same task. The things which help such an integration already initiated are many and varied.

Formation of a new community, single and homogeneous, by the destruction of the old ones is a difficult task. And the degree of success necessarily depends on the size of the task. If the two communities to be put together speak the same language, have the same religion, or belong to the same race, the task is comparatively easy; but if they differ in all these respects, the task becomes difficult.

The process of isolation and differentiation of the world's peoples has now almost come to an end. The process of the unification of the world has already set in. The discovery of America and of the sea route from Europe to India may be said to be the most important steps in this direction. This is the era of communication between countries, of exchanges in "civilizations," and of the intermixture of bloods. The whole world is tending to become homogeneous in ideas, customs and manners, and in what we may call "civilization."

In the process of unification what things have taken and will take the lead has differed and will differ according to the times and place. In some countries the propaganda of religions did great service, while in some other places political conquest has made the chief contribution. Political and religious conquests have been the most important factors, but not the only factors.

Political conquest merely makes one political body out of a number of distinct political groups. Political conquest does not necessarily lead to social integration. It often fails in making the community brought under one government a homogeneous nation. But very often this conquest accelerates the process. Let us see how it does.

First of all the political conquest tries to obliterate ruthlessly the past civilization. It often enforces its own religion on the conquered tribe. This factor was very potent in the past ages, but it is not so now. The conquest very often leads to the suppression of the language of the conquered by the language of the rulers. The patriotic element in the conquered country generally resents such change, but very often it has to acknowledge the defeat, and yield. The suppression of the native language and superimposition of a foreign one makes the conquering and conquered nation similar in thought and idea. The higher education is generally given in the language of the conquerors instead of that of the conquered, with the pretence that the languages of the conquered are not suitable carriers of the higher thought, science and culture. The administration is also carried on in the language of the conquerors.

Again, the conquered nations imitate the conquering ones. Generally the conquering race forms the aristocracy, and the imitation of them is governed by the same laws by which the imitation of the upper class by the lower class is governed. Even in a country where the foreign rulers are theoretically outcasts, there will be enough men from the native society who would imitate their rulers. Moreover, inasmuch as imitation is the best form of flattery, those who imitate the rulers are generally favoured by them. The persons who imitate without any scruples of self-respect are complimented by the ruling class as more progressive. This spirit of imitation is manifested not only in dress and manners, but even in religious form and ceremonial. If a nation is conquered by a race which secludes women, the conquered will also seclude their own women. If the women of the conquerors are free and bold, the conquered nation will try to remodel their relations between the sexes.

More than this. An appearance similar to the conquering nation very often saves individuals of the conquered nation from the personal insult and humiliation to which the members of the conquered nation are put. Imitation helps a person of the conquered race to pass as an individual of the conquering race.

The imitation does not always originate in flattery. Very often the conquered become conscious of the real superiority of the institutions of their conquerors and adopt them. The moral effect created by conquest is so great, that even the follies of the ruling race pass for virtue among the conquered, and the latter try to adopt them.

It is not very difficult for the invaders to impress on the mind of the conquered the superiority of their own god and their own religion. The conquered tribe often begins to feel that the god of victors is stronger than theirs, though they may often call the enemy's god a devil. If the conquerors belong to any particular theophratry, membership of that theophratry becomes an advantage to people from the conquered class who may join that theophratry. If the feeling of brotherhood be very strong, then the converts become united with the conquerors. If it is not very strong, then the new converts are treated contemptuously to be sure, but greater favour is shown to them than that shown to the people outside the theophratry.

Let us now try to estimate the importance of another cause which has contributed to modify civilization; and has led to the unification of a portion of the world. The factor referred to here is the propaganda of a religion. I have used the word religion not in the sense of philosophy or ideal of life, but in the sense of the entire system, like Christianity, which is popularly considered as religion. In fact, no strong missionary movement for religious conquest has been undertaken and achieved with an unmixed and honest desire of spreading higher ideals of life. The stress laid on the ethical ideas in religion and the ideals of life therein has been a very recent matter, and even now the ethical ideas have not been singled out for propaganda or for missionary work. That the people of old ideas almost identify barbarism and heathenism, that is profession of dissimilar religions, is not a mere accident; for the conversion to a different religion has helped to change the entire civilization. Let us be more concrete and see how such a process has taken place with reference to the spread of Christianity.

But before entering into a discussion of this topic the different items which a religion is composed of should be clearly indicated, to show what the conversion to a religion does really mean—what effect it has on an individual.

In order to estimate the effects of the propaganda of a system, one may well begin by ascertaining the effects of the components. Advocates of the propaganda of any certain religion often forget that the advisability of the missionary work of any particular religion is to be judged by the total effects which a transference of the system is likely to produce.

Let us see what Christianity is composed of. First of all, Christianity means discipleship of Christ, or acceptance of him as God or Son of God. This discipleship includes a number of ceremonies like baptism. It also includes observance of some festivals like Christmas and Easter. It also includes beliefs regarding the unknown, like God, devil, soul, heaven, and hell. Christianity does not include only discipleship of Christ, but also the Jewish tradition and biblical history. Nowadays many churches are beginning to proclaim that Christianity does not include belief in the Jewish history, but only in the apostolic faith. But if anybody observes the present condition of Christian churches, and of the attitude of the missions whether Protestant or Catholic, he will plainly see that the proclaimed profession is different from practice. The very fact that the Old Testament is included in the Bible will give the lie to the profession.

Acceptance of Christianity again involves negation of all that is not compatible with the ideas, spirit, institutions recorded in, sanctioned by, and approved of in the Bible. A good Christian should forsake all the old institutions of his tribe, nation, or race that is against the Christian scripture. The general effect of the conversion to the Christian religion then is not difficult to determine. It tries to efface almost all the tradition of his nation and replaces it with that which is Jewish or biblical. The produced effects never come anywhere near to the expectation. Many heathen institutions receive a Christian coating and become part of Christianity. Old heathen gods become saints of Christianity; and some of the old heathen customs become Christian customs. Still, some outward semblance of uniformity is produced. Again, as one nation adopts Christianity, it then spreads it in a modified form. Then, in fact, what that nation tries to do in its missionary work is to propagate the ideas and institutions of its own nation under the cloak of Christianity. A great part of European Christianity is derived from the Christianity of Greece and Rome. And with that Christianity, Greek and Roman institutions have been transferred. Latin and Greek have become almost sacred languages, though the original scriptures were perhaps in Hebrew, and though (as some scholars believe) Jesus himself spoke Aramaic. European nations now have accepted Christianity, and when they try to propagate it they do not try to propagate the ideas of Christ so much as they try to propagate the ideas and institutions of their own country, under the pretext of propagating Christianity. A clear example of this kind would be seen in India. In Southern India there is a custom of tying *tali* at the bride's neck.[1] Christian missionaries have an objection to this heathen article and wish to replace it by a ring, though the exchange of the ring itself is a relic of European heathendom. Even the abhorrence of the Hindus for

[1] See the word *tali* in Thurston's *Castes and Tribes in Southern India*, Madras, 1909.

liquor and animal food, which encourages destruction of life to satisfy the palate, was treated as a heathen prejudice; though fortunately, with the growth of higher ideas of morals, the Christian missionaries do not nowadays insist on taking away this part of heathenism from their converts.

Not only by trying ruthlessly to kill heathenism in its converts has Christianity tended to produce similarity, but also by promoting or creating a positive feeling of brotherhood. The Church insists that those who join the Christian faith are and should be considered as brothers. All the Christians again meet in church, and thus promote intercourse between the members of the theophratry. With the Christian population there are many things common. They have a common tradition, common holidays, common customs, a common master, and some common ideas. If the racial difference among men brought together under a common church is not too great, all the tribes become unified.

I have admitted that religions (theophratries) do exert a unifying influence, and still I have maintained that the religions are anti-social in their nature. These two statements should not be regarded as inconsistent. The process of contact has some advantages over religions. The process of contact does not oppose the idea of a territorial society, while the process of religions does. The process of religions tries to create a social group, based on belief and worship, and irrespective of the territory which the people may occupy. Thus, in fact, religion does more to disintegrate a territorial society than to integrate it. Those who wish to promote social integration in a certain territory, by creating nationalism or imperialism, should beware of these theophratries, which, as history has shown, are a curse to Humanity.

It is impossible to find a perfectly integrated society. Most of the existing societies are lacking in something or another to attain the ideal. As the process of the formation of the larger community by the union of the smaller is always going on, no time is left for the completion of the process of integration of any community. The difficulties of integration have been multiplied by the strange irony of fate which has subjected the groups of people to various and conflicting integrating influences. For example, the political dominion of one race has been extended over another race entirely differing from the first in language, manners and civilization in general. People speaking the same language and having the same manners are divided into different states. Peoples dissimilar to each other in race, customs and manners are professing the same religions; and people who resemble each other a great deal do not profess the same religion. Various religions are being followed in one state.

Though it is impossible to find a perfectly integrated society, it is still possible to describe some of the characteristics of the perfectly integrated society.

In a community where the process of integration becomes completed, the various races contributing to the formation of the community must become thoroughly mixed in blood, in their civilization and manners. The old racial feeling will at that stage entirely disappear, and will be replaced by the feeling for the combined community. Even the old racial consciousness must disappear, otherwise that consciousness will become the cause of sympathies and antipathies.

When the civilizations will combine the old divisions of labour will disappear and a redistribution of labour will take place. Old tribes, which in manners, customs and life may be different from each other, will have different wants. The producers for those wants will also be different. For example, two tribes which differ from each other will have different classes of tailors. Sometimes some commodities are consumed by one tribe and not by another. In such a case the class which produces those commodities will become connected with one tribe and will have very little to do with the other. Under a unified civilization the life of the descendants of the two tribes will be alike, and this change will cause a new reorganization of the division of labour.

Another characteristic of the unified civilization is that there will be common aristocracy. We may say that common aristocracy is non-existent when some section of the people regards some class as social head, while another section may deny it or even go to the extent of regarding the political head of the community, or social head of a section of the community, as an infidel or an outcast. It is not necessary that the political and social heads should be the same. Two different authorities in these matters may exist in a perfectly integrated community, but their prestige should be recognized by all the tribes brought under one political system.

Thus to a perfect integration of the society distinctions of various character in the population are injurious. The principal ones of them are :—

1. Differences in the worship of the peoples, differences in their theology, and in such of their systems of thought

as become hereditary in the population, being a relic of the old tribal culture.

2. Linguistic distinctions also keep the people apart, and become factors of disintegration.

3. Distinctions in manners and fashions, distinctions in the articles of consumption, and also other cultural distinctions are injurious to society, when they are due to the old tribal lines and therefore hereditary.

Some people appear to believe that the present multiplicity of castes and complexity of the system are a result of original good and simple conditions becoming worse. In fact, such a view has been held both by learned and ignorant. This is the view which pervades the writings of European scholars as well as those of Hindus. Christian missionaries have turned this belief to account by ascribing the growth of evils to Brahmanism, and have tried to make that wrong supposition an argument in favour of the propaganda of their own religion. To a person endowed with better knowledge of facts, and with ability to formulate some laws connecting and explaining those facts, the history of the past has an entirely different meaning. He would plainly see that the present conditions should not be looked upon as a degeneration of the good conditions of the former times, but only as a result of insufficient integration or insufficient unity of the groups that were brought into contact. Hindu society, that is, all people of India (excepting those who have joined foreign creeds and thus have become members of foreign society), disunited and divided into castes as they may seem, are far better united to-day than ever before. There have been a number of divisions of later growth, and some more divisions are taking place even to-day, but all these can be interpreted as by-products, and even necessary by-products, of efforts towards unification and equality. The history of caste in India is not then a history of the increase of social division and inequality, but a history of less rapid, or to use the popular but inexact word "arrested," development, arrested organization and arrested integration.

Thus, the name "History of Caste" itself becomes to a certain extent inappropriate. The proper name for the study would be a history of the development of Hindu society.

There is another reason to make the name "History of Caste" inappropriate. In a society the relations of classes and castes are affected and determined by political changes, religions, revolutions, economic changes, and also by changes in social philosophy. They are also greatly influenced by immigration of foreigners. Under these conditions the treatment of the caste system or any other social phenomena in an isolated manner is impossible. It is somewhat easy to isolate to a moderate extent any particular phase of social life at any given period; but if a writer is dealing with a period extending over three or four millenniums, the interconnexion of the phenomena becomes so great that the separation becomes well-nigh impossible.

Nevertheless, the name "History of Caste" will be maintained. Though I shall have to write a history of the development of the Hindu society and its civilization, an attempt will be made to give greater prominence to facts directly relating to social organization and distinctions, than to other phases of civilization.

A proper application of the factors which contribute to nation-making, or to use a wider term, of social integration, and a realization of their absence in India hitherto, would make clear the fact that the chief reason why all previous attempts, real or imaginary, honest or dishonest, have failed is because the time had not come. No reform for the abolition of caste system would have had any chance of success unless the whole of India was treated simultaneously by the reformer. Any simultaneous action would have been possible only when India should have been brought under one government, and under conditions when all the people of India should have felt their unity and should have had the opportunity of co-operating in the adoption of a uniform policy. More than this. Such a task calls forth men capable of influencing the whole country, with ability of managing vast empires, and with honest desire for social reform.

When I say that the time had not come I should not be construed to mean that the previous attempts were well meant and well directed, for a large number of them were not. Most of the so-called " religious reformers " were not men who were at all inspired by any motives of social reform. Some of them, whom European scholarship, often anxious to expose the folly of the Brahmans, has styled " religious reformers," were men inspired by motives no other than that of getting incense burnt before themselves ; some of them mendacious rogues, and some religious demagogues. Success in founding religions does not always require any great knowledge or a zeal for the improvement of the human lot, or even manly virtues. Very often, or almost always, the men who succeed are those who possess a great deal of audacity, impudence, appetite for honour, and capability for cheating, that is, for making miracles.

Some religious men or reformers were anxious to turn away the minds of their followers from material objects, and would have been glad to see the earth converted into hell so that the change may turn the human mind from the world and its pleasures towards something which they knew to be higher and permanent. It is almost foolish to expect any social betterment from the philosophers of this school. To add to these classes, there were some religious reformers who really wanted to make some important changes in the social organization. But these men played the parts of quacks and barbers instead of physicians and surgeons when they attempted to remedy the social evil.

However unpalatable it may seem to us, and however humiliating it may be to our pride, we should be prepared to confess that the greatest achievement done towards the integration of our society is achieved by a foreign race of invaders, who have succeeded in bringing the whole of India under one strong control, and who have compelled the various warring races and nationalities in the country to forget their feuds in common subjection. They have helped us not only by forcing a political unity on almost the whole of India, but by bringing to our door the products of Western civilization. They have made it possible for all peoples of India to come together and to know each other. Even the common hatred which we occasionally feel on account of some unwise actions of the representatives of that nation towards it, draws us nearer. More than this, we have come to realize what the abolition of caste system means by vivid and concrete examples of the European nations, the observation of which has become more possible for us. If we look behind we find that often those who championed the abolition of caste did not at all know what the abolition of caste meant. To a large number, these words simply meant only the suppression of the Brahmanical supremacy, which is in fact the least injurious part of the caste system.

But what does all this show ? It first of all gives us a strong reason to be optimistic. The abolition of caste is, then, not a superhuman task. " Reformers " of the past failed because their methods had been wrong and because the time had not yet come. Realization of this fact itself should give us ground for hope. Our efforts therefore have great chances for success, provided we do not commit the same old blunders which men from the times of Gautama to those of Ram Mohan Roy have committed. This task would, of course, require huge efforts, a sacrifice on the part of the upper castes, a larger philosophy of brotherhood, and many other kinds of efforts, guided by the help of social sciences yet to be created.

CHAPTER IX

FUTURE OF HINDUISM

"WILL Hinduism spread?" Before answering this question it is necessary to give to the expression some definite meaning. The question is capable of being interpreted in several different ways. We may interpret it as a question whether Hindu ideas will spread, or whether membership of Hindu society will be extended to others in future. It is possible to make an affirmative answer to this question provided we make it with a proper explanation of the meaning. The spread of Hinduism should not be understood in the sense in which we use the expression "the spread of Christianity." The spread of Christianity means increase in the membership of the sampradāya by recruits from other tribes; while the spread of Hinduism means carrying Hindu civilization to peoples not yet brought under Hinduism, so that the Hindus may regard those peoples as nearer to them than to any other peoples; and the other people also may think in a similar manner.

From the nature of Hinduism already described it will be clear that Hindus first of all have a conception that all the tribes and races in the world form one community composed of Brāhmaṇas, other Āryas (good, noble people; that is, Hindus themselves), and Barbarians, that is, the jungle tribes in India and the foreigners. When this theory is taken into consideration then, first of all, making non-Hindus into Hindus simply means raising the foreign races to the status of an Ārya.

How is this work accomplished? By contact merely. Take a number of Hindus, let them come into contact with uncivilized people, and become dominant among them. In the course of time the uncivilized tribes will adopt Hindu ways and manners and become what the world would call "Hindu low castes." Although this method has succeeded with uncivilized tribes, it has failed to "Hinduize" more cultured foreign races. It does not mean that Mohamedans and Christians in India do not resemble Hindus in manners, customs and ideas. In fact, they do, and yet the fact is that they do not consider themselves Hindus. For, the acceptance of the social system of the Hindu by them as their own would make them in theory simply low castes of the Hindu community. To uncivilized races there is no alternative, but that is not the case with Mohamedans and Christians. They have a desire to consider themselves apart from the Hindu community.

Hinduism does not make any distinction between refined Europeans and foreign civilized nations, like the Chinese and the Japanese, on one hand, and the savage tribes in India on the other, like Bhils, Todas, and Garos. They all are mlechchhas, or barbarians, for there is only one civilization in the world and that is Hindu or Brāhmaṇical; the rest are barbarisms, defilements, or practices of the excluded communities.

Under these circumstances there is only one method possible whereby members of respectable foreign communities could become members of the Hindu society, and it is by their joining the sampradāyas, like the Ārya-samāja and Brāhma-samāja, which open their doors to them. I have also seen some Mahānubhāvas converting one Mohamedan, and the Jains converting a Parsi to their fold. This door of the sampradāyas is at present the only door for civilized races to enter Hinduism, that is, to become members of the Hindu community. Yet there are other ways for the foreigners to get in which may become open later; but before they become so it is necessary to reform Hinduism. It may well be said here that however the Brahmins may blame the sampradāyas, specially those of the Ārya-samāja and Brahma-samāja, they may thank these for the above-mentioned service they render at present.

When we think of reforming Hinduism, that is, reforming the entire Hindu civilization, we shall have first to consider its drawbacks, and this is not an easy task. Still a few prominent defects may be noted.

The most important drawback of the Hindu social system is its lack of integration. Hindu society is divided into watertight compartments of over three thousand castes and of many more sub-castes. The result is disunion of the people, the worst type the world has ever seen. The sampradāya system of social organization, which has united castes and tribes, has achieved a unity of the people in Mohamedan and Christian countries by the rise of two strong sampradāyas. The sampradāyas in India have failed to achieve unity. It is not because the founders of the various sampradāyas were not men of the order of Christ or Mohamed; but the Indian sampradāyas have failed because the intellectual tradition in the country was so great and extensive that the sampradāyas appeared to be very narrow. Sampradāyas could not have given to the

Hindu world what the religions gave to the Western world. Ideas on epistemology, theology and other philosophies were given by religions to Europe, while India had all these without the sampradāya. For the same reasons Christianity and Mohamedanism have failed to eradicate the Indian philosophy and thought. Each of these foreign sampradāyas has absorbed men from the ignorant multitude, but the former did not appeal to the intellectual class, as the latter regard these religions as merely tribal and inconsistent cults with nothing new that is valuable. As the sampradāya system has failed, some new system needs to be devised.

But what is the cause of this lack of integration ? First of all, a philosophy which could teach the people to absorb tribes and nations into one strong nation was lacking. It has been shown that Hinduism did not produce any idea of nationality. They had only one conception of unity above the conception of jāti, and it was the conception of humanity. They had a conception of welding the whole of humanity into one people, divided into a hierarchy of four varṇas or classes, with the Brāhmaṇas at the top. This was their theory of the social ideal, but the way in which it worked was to create a society in India and in neighbouring countries, such as the islands in the Indian Ocean in Further India, perpetuating a number of castes hierarchically superposed, with the Brāhmaṇa at the top. The Brāhmaṇas' ideal was not to maintain castes but to maintain four varṇas or, if possible, only two varṇas, namely, Brāhmaṇas and the Shūdras. But this ideal has failed. The status of a Shūdra has not been flattering enough for all castes to lose their individuality under the name Shūdra.

Until the rise of Mohamedanism and the immigration of

Mohamedan tribes into India as conquerors, Indians had no consciousness of their distinctive character and they did not possess any distinctive name. They continued to maintain the theory of tribal hierarchy with the Brāhmaṇas at the top. Even after the Mohamedan conquerors came they did not give up the theory, but regarded Mohamedans only as a mlechchha or anārya jāti, that is, ignoble caste whose place is at the bottom of society. Now a Christian race has come to rule, but still the theory is not given up. Englishmen and other Christians are classed together among low and ignoble tribes.

Though the Hindus thus produced a universal social philosophy for themselves, the character of the philosophy has not been such as the world would accept. The Hindus again had not sufficient ability to force it on the world. For example, had the Indian princes coupled with Brāhmaṇic wisdom conquered the world, or had the Brāhmaṇas gone all over the world and become priests of the world, as they became priests of the Indians, then their social philosophy would have received universal recognition; but such a state of things never came into existence.

Again, Hindus did not produce any social philosophy which could unite them and inspire them with a mission, till the foreign sampradāyas came into India and threatened to sweep away its civilization altogether. All the tribes absorbed by the sampradāyas of Christ and Mohamed were inspired with such a philosophy and have succeeded in uniting a large number of people.

When we speak about any kind of reform in order to integrate the Indian people, we should have some kind of sociological theory giving us the conception of what we wish to achieve. Unless we have a clear conception of the same we cannot adopt any rational and systematic measures. That it is necessary to change Hindu society is something that may well be granted, but the question before us is what to conserve and what to destroy from the old and what new things we have to add. In order to undertake this eclecticism, what we have to do is to make some forecast regarding the future of the world's civilization, by examining its tendencies, and also to determine the possibilities of changing the world's civilization on desirable lines.

There is one idea which may pass uncontested, and that is making the entire world into a single community. The history of the world, whether of its politics or of its economics, or of its social intercourse, or of sciences and arts, will give enough evidence to show that a tendency towards this has been growing up since immemorial times. Formations of larger political bodies, extinctions of the unfit, formations of larger social units on the basis of sampradāya or religion, spread of superior civilizations have been contributing towards this end.

Thus, the chief work to be done for the reform of Hinduism is to create a society perfectly integrated, with a view that it may find a fit place in the cosmopolitan system.

One trait of human nature should not be forgotten, either in interpreting the past or in planning the future. We have often seen that those who aim at less achieve more. The feeling which Mohamedanism and Christianity have inspired is the feeling of brotherhood and equality of those who belonged to their creed. These two religions have to a large extent succeeded in their attempt. The philosophy which Hindus produced and disseminated was, in fact, far more liberal. Vedanta, for example, does not stop short at saying that all Hindus or all men are brothers. It goes further and teaches, " You and I are one." It inspires the feelings not of brotherhood and equality, but of identity and unity. Still, with a philosophy so liberal as this, no unity was created. A theory like the brotherhood of man or brotherhood in a smaller group, however intelligently explained by a philosopher, does not sway the multitude and affect their actions unless the multitude sees before it clear necessity for putting that theory into practice. This necessity may be created either by desire for plunder, defence, or propaganda of a god or doctrine. Thugs and missionaries of religions have generally a strong sense of brotherhood, as they have desire of stealing money and members respectively from outside groups. Mere cosmopolitanism would not unite the entire Hindu society. It would not weld the different castes and tribes into one group. In order to accomplish this ideal we want a somewhat narrow social philosophy, at least temporarily. This narrow philosophy should not be based on religious prejudices, or tribal feelings. What we should have is a territorial sentiment irrespective of religion or race. We want Indian nationalism, and Indian patriotism. It is the duty of the Indian poets, writers and statesmen to cultivate this feeling. When strong nationalism will make Indians feel that they all are one group with members connected with each other by ties of blood, tradition and interest, then only will come the time for cosmopolitanism to germinate and spread.

Thus the bases of Indian unity are these: Cosmopolitan philosophy in the matters of " religion " should be promoted, but while we make the effort to promote it in India, valuable service will be done to the entire world.

In political and social matters, the consideration of religion, god worship and so forth ought to be discouraged. Hindus will have to give up the social dogma that all Mohamedans and Christians are Mlechchhas. But as a pre-requisite of the dogma it would be necessary to create the idea of equality of all tribes.

In order to accomplish this equality the doctrine of purity and pollution will have to be abandoned.

In order to weld the different tribes together and prevent the continuance of the feeling of inequality the restrictions on marriage also must be removed.

All these changes again are to be accomplished in the orthodox manner, that is, without the creation of a new theophratry (sampradāya), or without the promotion of an existing theophratry.

To reform Hinduism is therefore to transform Hinduism into Indianism, or what is popularly called Indian Nationalism. This task is not an easy one. Simple newspaper agitation ringing the word "Indianism" or "Indian Nationalism" into the Indian ears, asking every Indian to call himself "Indian" and reject the more restricted group-terms like Maratha, Bengalee, Hindu, Mohamedan, or Parsee, is not likely to bring about the change. The question is not of the name, but of the barriers. In fact, Frenchmen and Russians are separated from each other by less social barriers than the Marathas and the Bengalees, though the latter groups may be anxious to be called by the name Indian, may even be proud of the name, and are united together by the ties of common interest, political and economic. Indians, in order to reach Nationalism, have to go through a process through which the Europeans have gone, but more rapidly.

In order to explain the steps through which the European nations have ascended to Nationalism it may be well to compare the European nations with the Indians. One factor which did more than anything else to help the formation of the European nations, is *the change from tribalism to territorialism* of society. The importance of this factor has not been sufficiently appreciated by the sociologists, with the probable exception of the late Dr. Morgan, of Rochester, N.Y. It is this change which more than anything else prevented the growth of caste system in Europe. Social tribalism and social territorialism should be sharply distinguished from political tribalism and political territorialism. When subjection to a political authority is confined to a roving tribe, it is political tribalism, and when political authority is extended over a certain area, irrespective of the tribes therein, then it is political territorialism. When jurisdiction in many social matters by a certain head is extended over people in various parts, and when the political authority does not interfere with such social usages of those peoples, then it is a social tribalism. The Roman Catholic Church is a fine example of social tribalism. British jurisdiction over the British subjects in Oriental countries like China and Persia, and in the Native states of India, is an example of political tribalism. When any people in a land are governed by laws and customs restricted to the tribe, and if the political authority there does not enforce those laws and customs, then it may be called a social tribalism. It is the duty of the lovers of equality to discourage such tribalism, and to create territorialism at the same time.

Territorialism is not the final stage in the human evolution. It is not irrevocable. There is always a danger to a territorial society of becoming a tribe. As a tribe has a tribal pride which makes them refuse an alliance with tribes which are regarded as inferior ones, so territorial societies after becoming nations develop national pride which makes the people proud and insular. In any country if several unassimilative social elements come, then the territorial character of the society is greatly in danger. The assimilative power of a territorial society is subjected to a great deal of tension when the immigrants in their country differ in complexion and other physical characteristics, in dress, manners, religion, and in other features of civilization. It is not unlikely that India may have developed territorial societies in various localities. But it is possible that those territorial societies may have again lapsed into tribes. Again, if we review the condition of societies in the world we do not find clean-cut divisions of tribalism and territorialism, but one merges into another. It is not the case that some countries have entirely territorial societies and some countries have entirely tribal communities. Still, some European nations like England and France and the Oriental Empire of the Japanese may well be considered as fair examples of territorial societies as one can find. The colonies and countries inhabited by the European nations have carried the territorial idea with them, but their ideals are being severely tested by the various races they come in contact with. The people of the United States are struggling hard to keep their territorial character. And it is likely that some day they will be able to surmount the difficulties in their way. On the other hand India may be singled out as an example of the most extravagant development of tribal community.

Let us consider the case of a nomadic tribe, with its own chief, its own customs or laws, and with its own aristocracy. Suppose this tribe occupies a territory with substantial permanence, leads a more settled life and develops agriculture and arts. See the difference which such a change may entail. The first change which is likely to be created is that it may make the assimilation of an individual foreigner easy. As long as the tribe is nomadic the chances of foreigners coming into the tribe are less, though they are not entirely non-existent. Such tribes often get individual men who may be refugees from a rival tribe ; or they may adopt kidnapped children or may enslave some outsiders. By these methods some foreigners come into their fold. But when they lead a more civic life the tribal laws and customs become territorial laws and customs. The chief of the tribe becomes the king of the territory and taxes foreigners and gives them protection. The foreign individuals often marry with the natives or citizens and become guided by the territorial laws, and thus become united with that territorial society.

The foreigners are often subjected to disabilities. They are denied some civic privileges, and their social life is often neglected. They are allowed to manage their own affairs, and are permitted to follow their own customs regarding, say, marriage inheritance, wills, etc. In a case of this kind the tribalism of the society is greatly preserved. But if the citizens create new laws by methods similar to that which gave rise to *Jus Gentium* among the Romans, that is, by selecting some laws and customs of the foreign tribes and execute those laws themselves among foreigners only, then the foreigners become more closely united with the body politic. If they subject themselves to the *Jus*

Gentium thus derived, then the distance between them becomes still less. If all the disabilities on the foreigners become removed, then the foreigners cease to be the lower class.

But, on the contary, if the foreigners are allowed to keep up their own customs and laws, the tribalism of the society becomes perpetuated and thus creation of a caste system is facilitated. Democracies are usually extremely intolerant regarding foreign ways and manners; for the greater the amount of difference the greater is the difficulty of assimilation.

The ultimate result of tribalism is plain. The existing tribes will be more or less perpetuated and will give rise to a caste system. It is an inevitable result, from which there will be no escape.

The territorial societies, like the Englishmen, Americans, etc., in themselves have no different future: if they do not keep themselves on guard they also will become tribal societies. As long as man is freely migrating it is not the present condition of the society, whether territorial or tribal, which determines its character, but the insistence on the ideal, territorial or tribal. The so-called Anglo-Saxon communities, that is, Englishmen and the white Americans (the latter in fact have no more right to be called Anglo-Saxons than the American negroes have), are now developing a pride of their own and are showing a tendency to become tribes.

Danger to territorialism means the concourse on the same territory of races and tribes which will not fuse. Inasmuch as the fusion of peoples depends on similarity, enumeration of the danger to territorialism means enumeration of those dissimilarities which have a strongly separating influence.

It may seem strange to some philosophers who believe in the monogenic doctrine that various peoples, though descended from one stock, should now refuse to mix. But there is no cause for surprise. It is indeed true that men differ from their neighbours very slightly. If we start to make our observations from Australia northward into different directions, reviewing the various native tribes of the islands in the Indian ocean on the way, going first through Siam, China and Japan to Kamschatka, and from there to America, and secondly, going from Ceylon to Kashmir and from there westward to England, it would be extremely difficult to tell where one ethnic type ends and the other begins. We may find the same gradual change in dress, customs, manners and beliefs. One people resemble their neighbours and the latter resemble the people dwelling further on. But if we take two extremes we may find a vast difference. The racial hierarchy of America is not without a meaning ; the status of various European and Asiatic races in America may roughly be said to be in proportion to the distance from the Atlantic. The reasons are not difficult to seek. During the early stages of human development and culture mankind migrated slowly, and thus differentiated very gradually, and has thus developed the differences, small indeed, if only neighbours are considered, but great if we compare two peoples living at a great distance. Had the concourse of races followed similar lines, that is, each race would have met with the neighbour and not the people greatly removed, and again had they moved to each other very slowly, giving time to produce uniformity, physical and cultural, then great race prejudices would not have been given rise to as they exist now.

Thus the cause of the race question and immigation

questions in the New World is the concourse of races and nationalities greatly removed from each other. This concourse has been abrupt. There was no preparation for mutual adaptation. The greater part of the world has been appropriated by a few nationalities of Europe. By this appropriation some highly civilized populations came into contact with barbarous peoples and with people whose civilization has been entirely different. Again, as the Chinese and the Japanese began to migrate they came in contact with white people differing from them in many ways. The differences between the people who thus come in contact have been so great that their mixing with each other has been greatly prevented.

Side by side with this concourse of the diverse racial elements there has been some change in the institutions, ideas and capabilities of the peoples.

First of all, man has become much more liberal. People of to-day do not demand so much similarity of life and belief as the people of former times. Savages and Hindus [the latter are in fact little different from the former] refuse to contract alliances on very small grounds. The European peoples of to-day do not refuse to inter-marry unless the physical and cultural differences are great and marked.

As time and civilization have progressed the assimilative power of the people also has progressed. I think there is no country on earth where the people have shown greater power of assimilation than the United States. How the Americans have succeeded in converting foreigners of various races into Americans is almost incredible to a person who has not visited that country. The Americans themselves trust their assimilative power so much that they allow their own government and institutions to be influenced by the foreigners staying in the country for five years or over, and this "free door policy" of theirs adds to their assimilative powers.

What is meant by the increase of assimilative power? It means making other people more like one's own, and preparing the mind of one's own people for the acceptance of the foreigners into one's own social group. It requires preparation on both sides. Foreigners and natives both need to be educated. Again, the preparation for one means preparation for the other. If the foreigners become easily like the natives, then the prejudice of the native towards the foreigner becomes greatly less. On the other hand, if the natives or the dominant community are willing to extend the membership of that community, socially and politically, to the foreigner, then the foreigner has greater incentive to adopt the ways and manners of the native or the dominant community. The greater the increase of the assimilative power, the less becomes the friction.

What is the ultimate end of the territorial system with free migration? It is this. Man will be more individualistic. He will be able to choose his own nationality irrespective of his birth. He will identify himself with the interest of the territorial community he resides in. There will be a great deal of similarity among people all over the world, which will enable a man born in one community to adopt the civilization of other communities in the world. The physical differences among men will also be either less or of less consequence. Inter-marriage will take place among all nations, religions and races. The social relations of the peoples in the world will thus be greatly simplified.

How to convert the Indian tribal societies into territorial

societies? I may say here that part of the work in this direction has been already done by the British Government. The High Courts in India have jurisdiction over certain territories; they enforce part of Hindu law equally on all castes and tribes living in the territory under their jurisdiction. But they also recognize some social customs peculiar to the tribe, and sanction them. Thus though something is done by the British Courts a great deal remains to be done. And why? Because the territorial system has not been sufficiently appreciated. The present political divisions of India have been absurd because they have been due to historic causes.

In order to convert the tribal society into a territorial society it is necessary to make political divisions in India agree as far as possible with the areas occupied by the dominant tribes. To my mind the divisions of India on the lines of languages are the best that could be devised. There are, of course, some castes and tribes which overlap into various linguistic provinces, but this cannot be helped. When such divisions are created and when the native communities in India shall have won self-government, as they are bound to win it in the near future, Indians will make a great deal of social legislation, which at present is practically non-existent. The growth of Indian society and of Hindu law is curtailed by the lack of new laws suitable for the needs of the people. The people are getting a better hearing now in legislative matters than in the past. To these social laws all the people in the territory will be subjected, and thus uniformity will be created in the population. At present the various societies in a territory are governed by tribal laws, but in future they will be governed by territorial law.

It is not likely that the British Government will undertake reforms like political divisions on linguistic lines of their own accord, but they should be compelled to undertake such reforms by proper agitation. Under the new arrangement it is inevitable that the dominant tribes in a province are likely to enforce their own ideas, customs and institutions, on the minorities and on the aliens. But this fact in itself should not be considered as a disqualification of the territorial system. Things of this nature do occur in every country. It is a necessary process of nation-making. The dominant community should try to compel uniformity. We should not forget that behind the nation-makings of European countries lies a woeful tale of religious persecutions, interdicts to certain modes of dress, to certain languages, to certain customs, and so forth.

The country may perhaps develop certain local peculiarities, but these local peculiarities are far better than tribal peculiarities, which keep barriers of greater permanence between peoples. The idea of Indian nationalism may also be trusted to create uniformity.

Another important factor which contributes towards nation-making is the creation of such an aristocracy as would be recognized all over the territory. It is this aristocracy which, even though it may create sharp classes, contributes materially towards the nation-making, that is, towards preventing the growth of a caste system.

One advantage which this aristocracy has is that every tribe in the country tries to get a chance to mix with the aristocracy. People from every tribe may feel themselves honoured if they have a chance of contracting inter-marriage with the aristocracy. Unless there is such an aristocracy there is very little motive for the members of various tribes to seek an alliance with people outside the group. Every tribe hating a sister-tribe and feeling its own self-sufficiency will not contract alliances with outsiders. In India, with all the work of the caste system, the formation of genuine aristocracy never took place. There is no caste in India with universal prestige except the castes of Brāhmaṇas. The Kshatriyas never formed a caste. The ruling families of various states in India belong to various tribes of several grades. The Rajputs are considered the highest among all. The Marathas also have good prestige. There are several princes who call themselves Rajput, but are not recognized as Rajputs, and there are several who are regarded merely as jungle chiefs. There are also some principalities which are ruled by men of very low caste.

India had and has various aristocracies, but these aristocracies have been either local or tribal. Take for example the caste of the Marathas. This is a caste divided into two classes, namely, the Kunbis and the Marathas. There is no sharp separation between them, to consider them two different castes. These classes dine with each other freely and occasionally inter-marry. When a Kunbi becomes educated, and begins to wear better dress, he calls himself a Maratha; and such a claim generally goes unchallenged unless he has any well-known blemish in the family like a descent from a bastard. Among Bengali Brāhmaṇas and Kāyasthas there have been what is called "Kulîna" families. There are several classes like the Khatris and the Rajputs in Northern India, both of whom claim to be Kshatriyas. But a caste or class of people of Indian prestige instead of tribal or local prestige never issued forth from Indian Kshatriyahood. In fact, Kshatriyahood never existed either as a class or caste; it existed only in idea. It was only the Brahmanical theory that such a class exists. The theory of four varṇas has been an ideal to which the society, according to the Brāhmaṇa ideas, ought to conform. Hindu military classes failed to federate and therefore failed to create a class or caste that is universally respected. The only sources which could have helped to create a class which could dominate above all, and thus help to unite the communities, are political authority and sacerdoce. The political authority under Hinduism has failed in this attempt. After the overthrow of the Hindu princes by the Mohamedans the Hindu princes and the chiefs lost a great deal of their prestige, but the leadership of the Hindus instead of passing to the new political authority, namely, Mohamedan rulers, passed almost entirely to the Brāhmaṇas. Mohamedans were not regarded by the Hindus as their social head, but were regarded simply as out-castes who have taken the political authority by force. The Hindus, instead of thinking themselves honoured by intermarriage with Mohamedan rulers, would regard themselves as fallen and degraded if they were compelled to contract a marriage with this impure race. The same thing may be said of the English. The English cannot play the part of the social aristocracy of India as long as they are regarded as impure by the Hindus, and unbelieving idolaters by the Mohamedans.

Can a class be formed out of Indian princes, chiefs, and other potentates? In my opinion it is possible to create such a class and to use that class to unify India. It would also be desirable in many ways to make the princes, instead of the Brāhmaṇas, the head of the society from many standpoints which may be explained later. But such a task would need a great deal of education, sense of duty, and activity; things which have not been the characteristics of the Indian princes. They are filled with family pride, and appear to be incapable of any united action.

If the Indian princes level distinctions among them of tribe and family, and form a class among themselves which would freely intermarry and assert their own superiority over the Brāhmaṇas, it is possible for them to do so. I shall be but too glad to see the princes unite and challenge the supremacy of the Brāhmaṇas. The princes have wealth and power in their favour, the Brāhmaṇas have nothing but intelligence, education and accumulated prestige. But the princes have not as yet shown any ability to unite. It is known that the daughter of an important Indian prince was compelled to be a second wife of another prince of her own tribe, being unable to make a suitable match with a prince outside her own tribe. If the Indian princes unite they may be able to form a class, union with whom would be sought by people from all castes and tribes in India. It is not possible that the Brāhmaṇas will refuse to inter-marry with the princes, whatever their caste pride may be. Cases of Brāhmaṇas who considered themselves honoured by marriages with princes have occurred in the past. Cases of this kind occur even now. A prince in Eastern India, who belonged to a tribe regarded among the Hindu princes as merely low-caste jungle people, was able to marry a girl from a caste supposed to be much higher than his own. He was again able to find a Brāhmaṇa to marry his daughter when she was coupled with a dowry of one hundred thousand rupees.

Though we have cases of Brāhmaṇas who would rather

lose their hereditary Jaghirs than confer vedic sacraments on a Hindu prince who, in their opinion, was not entitled to them, still, men of such conservative spirit, who will always sacrifice worldly prospects to principle, will fortunately or unfortunately be always few. Most of the Brāhmaṇas are worldly men who would be influenced by money and power.

Unfortunately the princes with ability to take initiative in overthrowing the power of the Brāhmaṇas and to do constructive work in uniting India have not made their appearance. A large number of Hindu princes shower curses on Brāhmaṇas and do nothing more. In fact this has been the method of the Hindu princes who wanted to rebel against the authority of the Brāhmaṇas since the days of Gautama and, perhaps, long before that. Indian princes and other non-Brahmanical communities in India have been simply indulging in a cheap and irresponsible sedition against the Brāhmaṇas, the only uniters of Hindu communities. The princes seem to wish for prestige without responsibility and work; as long as they want this, the unity of India through their agency is a hopeless task.

If the princes are unable to play the part of Indian aristocracy, the Brāhmaṇas must play it. The Brāhmaṇas have some advantages peculiar to themselves. They are the only community in India whose position has always been at the top. Dynasties of princes have risen and fallen, but the Brāhmaṇas have remained unmolested. Nevertheless the Brāhmaṇas as they are will not be able to achieve any results. They should organize themselves. Every Brāhmaṇa caste should organize itself and affiliate to the others. When the Brāhmaṇas become organized they will acquire the power of deciding as to who should be members of their community. They will be able to exclude some of those who are already in the community and will also be able to extend the membership of their sacred circle to people from other castes whom they would consider fit. Brāhmaṇahood has many defects. The greatest of all defects is its tribalism. They are subdivided into about eight hundred sub-castes which do not inter-marry. A number of those divisions have been territorial in their origin, but now they have become tribal. Suppose a Kānyakubja Brāhmaṇa comes to Deccan, he has no chance of being regarded as a Dākshiṇatya. That Kānyakubja Brāhmaṇa has to go back to Kanoja to seek a wife, and his children in the Deccan will have to do the same when they want to marry. Pancha Gauda Brāhmaṇas and Pancha Dravida Brāhmaṇas, which were once only territorial divisions, have now become tribal divisions.

This is not the place to inquire as to why and how these various distinctions arose among the Brāhmaṇas. But some of the causes which convert territorial society into tribal society may be considered here. The first and most important reason has been mutual suspicion. When a man from northern India comes to southern India, and calls himself a Brāhmaṇa, many Brāhmaṇas in the south would suspect his claim and would have no connexion with him. The suspicion has its causes. Many cases of deception of this kind can be gleaned from folk-tales. Again, the ways of the northern Brāhmaṇa are different from those of the southern Brāhmaṇas, and the most important of the differences have been in the conception of what is pure and what is impure. For example, if a Brāhmaṇa from Gujerath comes to the Deccan and shows no scruples about drinking water from the hands of a non-Brāhmaṇa, the customs of his country permitting such a conduct, a Maratha Brāhmaṇa may exclaim, " What kind of Brahmaṇa is he, who drinks water from the hands of a Shūdra ? " He would thus begin to regard him as a person less pure than himself. Under these circumstances intermarriage is impossible.

I do not care to go into many details just now in the way of remedies to modify the caste system. I have only dwelt on such points as I consider to be the greatest obstacles to the nation-making and to contribute more than anything else to maintain a system of castes. The question of social reform will be made a special subject of treatment, as I may find time and opportunity to dwell on the subject. The obstacles which I have described to the nation-making of India have by no means been exhaustively enumerated. But I have given them only to make the reader see the past of the Hindu society in a different light.

CHAPTER X

FUTURE OF "RELIGIONS" AND THE UNITY OF CIVILIZATION

THE two sampradāyas of Christ and Mohamed also are struggling with each other, both with the idea of uniting the entire world by bringing it under their own brotherhood. Both of these are again struggling against the process which led to the formation of Hinduism.

The expansion by the process of sampradāya, of uniting races for the purposes of sampradāya, must cease some time. It is impossible to make all Christians Mohamedans, or all Mohamedans Christians. Therefore some other social philosophy larger than the philosophy of these sampradāyas (that is, loyalty to the particular religion) is needed, and to that philosophy the two religions, as well as the various Indian sampradāyas, should be subordinated.

What is that philosophy? It is the philosophy of "Mānava-dharma," which Hindus once tried to create and have failed. But some such principles of that philosophy which have been laid down will remain.

Those principles have been already discussed in a previous chapter. They are mainly the following:—

(i) Perfectly pantheistic doctrine regarding the nature of God.

(ii) Immateriality of the name of the deity and of the method of worship.

(iii) Universal supremacy of the doctrine of dharma, that is, supreme importance to the principles of morals, conduct and duty; which may teach the subordination of the interest of the smaller group to its duty towards the larger group.

(iv) Discouraging the formation of strong theophratries (sampradāyas).

What is then the future of the sampradāyas of Christ and Mohamed and of other sampradāyas in India? This is impossible to predict with accuracy, but the tendencies seem to be in the following direction.

These sampradāyas will not remain the determinant of social groups. The sampradāyas and their sects will continue to have members, but their membership will not affect the social relationship of men very much. They will simply become bodies of worshippers coming and meeting on the prayer days. But the amount of social intercourse between men will depend on other considerations. Even in the question of morals the scriptures of the sampradāyas will not become final authorities.

In the meantime Hinduism will develop into a better cosmopolitanism than it is now. The religions will take the same place in this cosmopolitanism as the sampradāyas have taken under Hinduism. That is, the world will have a common civilization, a more common idea of morals, and every one will be expected to fulfil his duties as a member of humanity. The religions may ultimately become only of ritualistic value, and even the ritualistic side may also disappear, in case the state inspires a sufficient feeling of sanctity in their marriages. Religious bodies will then become merely prayer societies, or societies for mutual help.

ARE THE RELIGIONS NECESSARY ?

When I say that the religions will disappear, a question may be asked whether religions are necessary for society. I may say frankly that they are not. But to prevent misunderstanding I should add some explanation.

The moral principles which the religions inculcate have done their service. They have contributed to the moral thought of the world, and a great deal of their contribution will remain and continue to guide society. Even ideas like Heaven and Hell or Nirvana may remain and will be of some use for the ignorant. Even the sense of mystery which all beings have may also remain, but what is unnecessary for society is the formation of a tribe with a separate social existence, believing all the ideas embodied in scriptures.

Hinduism, which is merely a tradition of the federated tribes, differs from bibliolatries like Christianity and Mohamedanism, in so far as the constitution of the United States differs from the English tradition or the so-called "British constitution." Every generation receives ideas and customs, as they come to them, modifies them and leaves them to future generations in a modified form. Different tribes come and mingle, exchange their traditions, and thus form a common tradition.

There may be ceremonies for conversion to religions (sampradāyas), to fraternities, to secret societies, to the sacred circle of the twice-born; but no ceremonies are required to initiate a person or a group of persons into tradition. Acquirement of a foreign tradition is a slow and unconscious process, and the acquirement of Hindu tradition by less civilized tribes has come into existence in this way; and when Brāhmans and the Brāhmanized Hindus were spreading their traditions they also borrowed the ideas and the traditions of the less civilized tribes.

The work for the future for Hinduism to perform is the creation of a mānava-dharma, common tradition for the whole world, a task which it once attempted, but with very limited success. The course of development in Western Asia and in Europe has been different from the course of development in India and Eastern countries. Once the entire Hindu civilization was in process of spreading itself over the whole world, and was going to accomplish a unification of civilizations in the world. But this course was arrested by the rise of "religions," the great dividers of mankind. These two Semitic religions sharply differentiated themselves from each other and both from the rest of the world, and thus made mutual understanding of men more difficult. When the Europeans saw the workings of the ancient process in India they called it Hinduism, and wrongly regarded it as a "religion."

The process of the creation of a common tradition for India and for the Western world has already begun. The results can be observed to-day. As far as India is concerned the results are as follows:—

(*a*) There has been a general tendency towards the decrease of the strength of ideas regarding ceremonial purity and pollution.

(*b*) The truth of the old beliefs and ideas has been suspected, and an attempt is made to discover the truth with the help of modern sciences or by appeal to the authority of modern scientists.

(*c*) On account of the new ideas and pressure of the new economic conditions the family life of the Hindus is changing. Polygamy is becoming extinct (*d*) A change is taking place in the dress, manners, and diet of the Hindus.

(*e*) Atheism and agnosticism and materialism are increasing in strength.

(*f*) The racial pride, which induced the Hindus to look upon the rest of the world as savage and impure, has considerably decreased, or at least been wounded. A large multitude of people have learned to fear and to hate the Europeans. Respect for the knowledge and the science of Europeans has increased. On account of the efforts of Christian missionaries, hatred for Christianity has also increased.

(*g*) A large number of stories from history (Epics, Itihāsa) and antiquity (Purānas) are now being regarded as myths.

(*h*) The ancient Hindu sciences and philosophies are now studied in a different light. With the dogma that "there is only one truth" (that there can be no contradictory orders of truth), an attempt is being made to reconcile the two different developments of sciences.

The production of common tradition for the whole world has been rendered to-day easier not only on account of the recent changes in Hindu thought but also on account of the development of European thought along the lines which India had already drawn over fifteen centuries ago or even long before. To a Hindu, looking carefully at European theology and philosophy, the occidental world seems just emerging out of theological barbarism. The noble ideas on theological matters which Hindus have once thought out are being appreciated now by the occidental thinkers, but in general the European world seems to be incapable of understanding their full bearing on account of either theological bias or lack of the intellectual preparation essential to understand a higher philosophy. Even to-day those great thinkers of Europe whose reasoning has led to ideas similar to those of the Hindus are not approved of by the European piety.

European thinkers have now begun to realize that the practices which they censure as idolatry do not differ in nature from their own practices.

They also feel that God did not reveal Himself specially to any particular tribe to the exclusion of the rest.

The theology of the Bible, and specially diabolism, has fallen into disrepute. The conception of God is much enlarged, the personal idea of God is being gradually abandoned, the conception of soul, as something peculiar to a man which other animals do not have, is regarded as an antiquated idea.

The effect on the West is noticeable also in its acceptance of items from Hindu philosophy. Buddhism and Buddhistic philosophy are making headway in Europe and America. There are in the West some believers in the Vedanta philosophy also. Hindu sacred books and great religious teachers in India have acquired a certain amount of religious veneration in the West.

Knowledge of Sanskrit and of psychological and linguistic affinities has made the occidental peoples realize that the Hindus are of the same branch of the Caucasian race as they are; and they have realized what they owe to India.

The influence of the Hindus has been much less on the West than that of the West on the Hindus. The reason for such a state of things is not difficult to see.

First, Europeans are politically dominant in the world: and the ideas whether right or wrong, and the customs whether wholesome or injurious of the dominant race prevail.

Secondly, India being a subjugated country has no separate political existence. It cannot therefore do much towards contributing to political morals.

Moreover, India being out-distanced by Europe in sciences, the day when the Indians will make their contribution to sciences is yet to come; still it will be admitted that the beginning has been made. European civilization has more to give to, than to receive from, the Indian civilization.

When I speak of the unification of civilization I do not mean that all the world will be entirely alike, for that condition would be evidently impossible, as the physical conditions of the various parts of the world vary greatly. Still by the contact of civilizations a great deal may be done to produce some common civilization. In the development of civilizations of localities and nations, whatever is wanting in one may be supplied by another. Less efficient methods and arts would disappear before those which are more efficient.

There is one factor of civilization which is capable of reaching unification earlier than the rest; and it is likely to influence all other factors. It is the knowledge and thought of the world. The primary dogma in this matter is that there can be no two contradictory orders of truth. To a great extent the stage has already come. Many sciences which are greatly cultivated by the Western world are freely accepted by the Oriental world. There can be no Oriental chemistry or physics different from the European chemistry, or physics which would hold contradictory opinions.

Still to-day there is a great deal of conflict in the ideas and beliefs of the various peoples. That conflict exists in those cases where truth is unknown; this conflict has been manifest specially in theological matters. It is possible to arrest this conflict and ill-feeling caused thereby, by promoting in the world the feelings and ideas of the educated Hindus.

The attitude of an educated Hindu towards the question of doctrine and worship is this. What God is is not entirely knowable, as it is an infinite conception. Of this infinite conception only a fraction in the form of an idea of either power, miracle or material, comes to the knowledge of man, by an occasional and wonderful manifestation. It is vain for a man to be proud of any particular manifestation and to exclude the rest from cognizance. All worship, therefore, should be tolerated. Any deity may continue to be worshipped provided the worshippers' conception becomes widened. It is neither proper nor necessary to replace one deity by another, because it is not a matter of importance whether the absolute and infinite conception is called Shiva Vishnu, Durgā, or Buddha. Whether a man worships the Sun, Jupiter or Saturn, or any historical great hero, or a saint or rivers like the Ganges or any other object that inspires awe or creates fear, is a matter of no importance. All these gods or manifestations are but starting-points. To disturb the faith of a man in a finite God is foolish as long as his mind is not fit to accept the higher. Pantheistic monotheism, which is the only possible form of consistent monotheism, is a very difficult conception to hold, as it taxes the mind to understand very difficult and mysterious laws, most abstruse philosophy and synthesis of most abstract concepts. Complete realization of this monotheism will negative the faith in sin and virtue, and this stage of mind if unaccompanied by other preparation of mind will result in an evil both for the individual and for the society.

The tendency of the world is to make the belief or cult of less consideration as the former and the determinant of the social group. The entire world will become one community. The moral ideas of men will become uniform. There would be a large stock of customs common to the whole world. The great sages of India, Arabia or Judea will become objects of more or less universal reverence among the intelligent classes of mankind. The ideas regarding the hereafter and unknown will be regarded simply as "beliefs" and not as dogma, which everybody must believe. There will be perfect toleration in these matters as it always existed and exists in India. The religious customs in different countries will continue to be practised, but they will be regarded as antiquity and tradition and will be followed only for the enjoyment they give. In this manner the chief aim of the process which formed Hinduism will be finally accomplished.

Appendix I

ON THE PRINCIPLES OF SCIENTIFIC STUDY OF RELIGIONS

Is "religion" a science? The answer to this question will depend on our definition of "science." If by "science" we mean only a systematic study, any phenomena in the world may be a subject-matter for a science; on the other hand, if we mean by that word a rational division of knowledge, then "religions" do not form a science. Though a separate place cannot be given to "religion" (?) or to religions, still it is possible to make a scientific study of them.

In the scientific study of any phenomena what is necessary to do first of all is to analyse the compound phenomena into their ultimate factors, and then the former should be explained in terms of the latter. This principle must be followed at the beginning to the rigorous exclusion of every other. But unfortunately this has not been the method of students.

Many Western scholars have attempted to define "religion" by what is called comparative and historical methods. They have ignored the popular meaning of the word and have tried to abstract their definitions from the comparison of Christianity on one hand and other systems like Hinduism, Taoism, Shintoism on the other, taking for granted that these systems are "religions." Their cry had been to abstract "religion" from "religions." A definition so abstracted would necessarily differ from the popular meaning of the word which I have already given in the formal definition. I do not condemn their definitions because they differ from the popular meaning of the word. I condemn them because their deduction has been erroneous.

The first principle of a scientific study is that the phenomena themselves should be studied by a proper analytical method before risking a grouping of various phenomena and then from definitions. A student should first try to make a proper analysis of the phenomena and should define each factor or component, and then he should define the various compound phenomena in terms of the components. He should classify the phenomena irrespective of popular nomenclature, for the popular nomenclature is based on superficial observation. A scientist is then expected to make his own nomenclature, classification and definitions. This process has already been adopted by the biologists ; for example, popular nomenclature would include whale and dolphin under fishes, but no biologist would include them in that class, making his definition of "fish" so as to suit that nomenclature. What is true about the nomenclature in biology is also true about that of sociology. When travellers visited other countries, or students in Europe named foreign systems of worships or philosophies, they unhesitatingly called them "religion," as they had some features common to the occidental conception of "religion." The observation had been superficial. Again it was unorganized, that is, one writer who called a particular foreign system a religion had one idea of religion or essence of religion, while another writer had another. As a result of this, almost entirely distinct types of systems were classed under the same name. It is no wonder that there should exist innumerable definitions of religion when the polymorphic phenomena were not studied by themselves. The students incautiously assumed that these phenomena are similar, and began to seek for uniformities.

In fact, if all the so-called "religions" were placed side by side and studied by a studious scholar it would have been impossible to arrive at any definition at all. Some definitions given by the "comparative and historical" scholarship exist only because the so-called "religions" have not been studied by them exhaustively. I can say without the fear of any contradiction that there is no scholar on earth to-day, nor ever has been, who has sufficiently mastered the most important civilizations on earth, in order to be able to compare their so-called "religions."

The idea of comparing a particular system with various radically polymorphous systems in order to understand the nature of that system is absurd in itself. To study other civilizations like the Hindu, Chinese, Celtic, Greek, Latin or Japanese with a complex notion like "religion" is something like studying the mineral products of another country with the help of chemical compounds found in your own country in a natural state, instead of studying them with the help of the elements.

Possession of scripture, ideas of God or future life, moral ideas, astrology, medicine, the principles of the formation of social group, strongest sentiments in the governing life of a higher type are factors that are capable of various combinations. The word religion represents a particular combination the nature of which I have already defined. If in any civilization this combination is found, then that combination may be called a religion; if that combination is not found, then any other combination should not be called a religion. So in some civilizations "religions" may exist, in some others they may not exist.

The concept of religion may be useful, to study other civilizations or general social science, according as other civilizations may or may not have the prescribed combination.

When I say that some civilizations may not have religions, it should not be considered as a censure of those civilizations, because the existence of systems called "religions" in a civilization does not mean a great compliment to that civilization. It is simply recognition of the existence of a particular combination.

Though the concept of "religion" may or may not be useful to general social science, it may be useful while dealing with European civilization. I am writing this work in English, but if I were to write a work in any other language, say like Marathi or Hindi, to interpret the occidental civilization I should leave the word "religion" untranslated just as the Europeans would leave the word *obeah* untranslated when they interpret the civilization of West Indian negroes.

A question may be asked: As very often one hears of

" religion " as a science with a special field of its own, and those scholars who have held this attitude have made useful researches, what place then does the study designated by that title occupy under the arrangement which I have suggested ?

The studies which have been conceived of as belonging to the " science of religions " belong to various types, and the different types of studies may be classed under different sciences. There are men who regard " religions " as merely social products, and study of religions as merely a study of social products. They hold that religions are results of man's interpretations of nature, of his attitude towards it, affecting and affected by his interpretations of the ideas of the life after death which may affect his conduct, by giving rise to ethical ideas, of conceptions of a superior object or powers real or unreal, like gods and devils. But there are also thinkers who do not regard " religion " as a science dealing with phenomena which are merely social products. They hold that religion is a science with a separate field which does not fall within the domain of the sciences already recognized. They hold that religion is not a science dealing with man's ideas regarding the occult and the mysterious, but a study of the occult itself. They in fact identify " religion " and theology and its kindred sciences. When Spencer assigned to science and religion the field of the knowable and unknowable, he had the same idea in mind.

My attitude has been different. I have held that " religion" and " theology " are not identical. Theology should include the scientific study of the occult and the absolute. Theology is a science either very old or very young. It is a most ancient science, because since very primitive times ideas on the subject have existed. It is a very modern science, because scientific research regarding the occult world, equipped with a desirable amount of scientific scepticism is just being thought about. A study of the ideas regarding god, of the various religions and peoples of various ages is a study of the history of theology. Study of religions means study of particular systems like Christianity, Mohamedanism and Buddhism, treating them as social products.

I have thus recognized theology as a science with a special field of its own, and I have distinguished it from "religion." I deny the name religion to theological science and reserve it for some special social products. The reason for the procedure is this—

At the very beginning we should sharply distinguish between two different studies, namely, (1) The study of systems like Christianity, and (2) the study of things which those systems teach or express opinions on.

The matters on which "religions" dwell or express opinions are many and various. I think there is hardly any department of knowledge on which the ancient books revered by religions do not have something to say. Every "religion" teaches something regarding ethics, astronomy or hygiene, but scientific investigations into any of these spheres of knowledge cannot be classed under the science of religion. Similarly a research for knowledge of Absolute things or of future life is not a science of religion, but is a subject-matter for theology.

Admitting that theology may be recognized as a separate science, not identical with the "science of religion," a question may be asked, as to whether a separate branch can be assigned to the study of the field under that arrangement which regards "religions" as merely social products. Those who have understood the previous argument regarding the nature of the phenomena embodied in religions, will answer the question for themselves. As the various factors of civilization are capable of various combinations, and religion is merely one particular type of combination, not necessarily found in all civilizations, there can be no science of religions. Religion is a compound available in too limited an area to be given a prominent place in the classification of sciences.

The only rational procedure for study would be to study each civilization separately, and also to study all primary concepts or elements in civilization, which are likely to be common to all. For example, worships, thoughts regarding the nature of divinity, ideas of morals, etc., of various peoples can be studied together and can form a branch of the social science.

Expressions like " origin of religion " should be forbidden in scientific writings ; though one may with propriety write upon subjects like " origin of worship," or " origin of the conception of divinity," or the origin of moral ideas. While studying these things comparative method may be of value.

Appendix II

ETHNOLOGICAL CLASSIFICATION AND ITS PLACE IN THE HISTORY OF MAN

THE question of the classification of sciences and of the materials of a science is already so much discussed that it has come somewhat under reproach. Notwithstanding this, I intend to dwell here upon the classification of the materials of ethnology. The theoretical aspects of this science are not in my opinion properly exploited. It is my belief that much needs to be done in this line in order to make the science rest on sure foundations.

Ethnology is, first of all, a science auxiliary to the history of mankind. It has to face questions for which one may or may not find information in written records. The general impression which an average student has is that it is a science which treats mainly of the classification of human races. If the aim of this science is primarily the classification of races, then classification itself would be regarded the end and not the means. But inasmuch as we conceive of ethnology as a science auxiliary to history, we shall have to admit that the classification is not the aim but only the means for the greater inquiry, namely, the history of mankind. If we keep this idea steadily in mind, we get an important principle, viz., whenever there are rival classifications of races before us, that classification which is of greatest historical value should be preferred.

Before carrying the above premise to its logical extent, it will be worth while to take into consideration the previous ideas on the subject of classification. The orthodox idea on the subject is that a scientist should not start in the study of his science with *à priori* notions, but should study the materials by themselves and should perceive the resemblances and differences in the materials, and should proceed to those conclusions where the former will lead. For some time this principle was regarded as the most important of all principles of method in natural sciences. When Comte laid down his system of positive philosophy he regarded the above idea as almost the primary dogma of positivity. Filled with admiration for the progress of biological science, he gleaned from that science, as it existed in his times, the above principle, and presented it to the students of other sciences with his compliments. He says, "We may derive encouragement from the example set by recent botanists and zoologists whose philosophical labours have exhibited the true principles of classification, viz., that the classification must proceed from the study of things to be classified and must by no means be determined by *à priori* consideration. The real affinities and natural connections presented by objects being allowed to determine their order, the classification itself becomes the expression of the most general fact. And thus does the positive matter apply to the question of classification itself as well as to the objects under it. It follows that the mutual dependence of sciences, a dependence resulting from that of the corresponding phenomena, must determine the arrangement of the system of human knowledge."

Even to-day a large number of biologists hold the principle enunciated above as the cardinal doctrines of scientific study. As this principle is not given up, and as classification has been hampered by an attachment to it, the teachings of that doctrine should be properly scrutinized. Let us inquire what expressions like "*à priori* consideration," "the real affinities" and "natural connexions" mean. Should we interpret the above admonition regarding the impropriety of "*à priori* consideration" as a prohibition of any tentative theory while working in the science? Personally I cannot interpret it in any other way, and I do not believe that the present scientists or philosophers would be at all willing to endorse this precept. Again, I wonder, how the so-called "real affinities and natural connexions" can be discovered unless we have already a certain system of ideas regarding the reality of affinities and naturalness of connexions.

The principle which Comte has laid down is not a principle which should be followed if we have any aim to lead the science to perfection. In fact, when the sciences are in their primitive condition the general tendency of the students is to examine the material by itself and try to arrange and to see to what valuable conclusions it may lead. When two affinities or connexions come before a scientist then he begins to ask which affinity or connexion should be preferred to the other.

In fact, what Comte has said regarding the method should not be regarded as a valuable precept for scientific inquiry but only as a procedure which a student of a science follows of necessity when he is unguided by any system of philosophy. If this fact is kept clearly in view, the difference between the method that is followed and the method that ought to be followed may be easily understood.

A science is generally approached from two different directions. The attention of some students is attracted by certain problems to be solved, while others are attracted to a certain material. While studying the material, problems arise, tentative theories are formed, and for the further study of those theories more materials are searched for. Geologists and biologists were at first drawn by the material, namely, the objects existing in the body of the earth and the living flora and fauna. When the theory of evolution was supplied to them, they began to speak of "the history of the earth" and of "historic geology" and so forth. Similar has been the case with anthropologists. Their attention was first directed to the systematization of material in the form of different races and civilizations of mankind. For the progress of knowledge both of the ways of approaching a science are necessary.

A clear perception of the distinction between the problem and the material and of their place in science will raise the question whether sciences are to be classified and named according to the material to be studied or the knowledge resulting from the material. I call attention to this question here for the benefit of those who may feel interested in discussing questions of this nature. For the actual knowledge of facts and for the solution of problems, immediate attention need not be paid to this question. Research may be carried on irrespective of any reform in the classification.

Though the question of the classification of sciences may be postponed for the present, the question of the classification of materials of a single science cannot be laid aside. The question of the classification of different fauna and flora is of the greatest importance to a biologist. As the question of the classification of the races of mankind is a serious one for an anthropologist, some attention to that question is imperative.

In the year 1859 two important works on the philosophy of biology appeared in both hemispheres. In America Professor Agassiz published his *Essay on Classification*, while in England the famous work of Darwin on the *Origin of Species* made its appearance. In the latter famous work we find a chapter on classification which is of permanent value to biologists and anthropologists. On the other hand, the essay of Agassiz, which represents the thought of the old school, has a singular flaw which makes the whole essay of questionable value. Agassiz never got rid of the notion of the immutability of species and refused to accept the theory of evolution. This essay is again vitiated throughout by his theological ideas. All that Agassiz explained is that while using the comparative method it is necessary to observe and compare a large number of things in the organisms under consideration. He was content to observe similarities and differences, but as he did not have any principle to test the importance of variations, we have found that the classification of Agassiz has become of almost no value to a modern student.

The great defect of the science of ethnology which I have pointed out previously is that the ethnologists are not able to agree on the classification of human species when they classify its members according to the present differentiations and variations. They are not able to offer any principle to judge the value of different variations. A large number of biologists show the same confusion.

Confusion in this matter is due to the inadequate and suspicious acceptance of the theory of evolution. Evolutionary theory has not yet been daringly applied to classification. The principles of classification consistent with the theory of evolution have been already enunciated by Darwin over sixty years ago. The application of the theory of evolution consists primarily in the classification of present species in the light of the past. If a number of species have been descended from a particular species of ancient times, all the descended species should be grouped together ; similarly in anthropology. If a number of tribes have come into existence as the result of the division of one original tribe, all these descended tribes should fall in the same category. This I consider as the first principle of anthropological classification, and it should be upheld, in my opinion, to the rigorous exclusion of every other rival principle. All the evidence derived from linguistic affinities and physical similarities is of very little value, unless it gives us a clue regarding common descent.

All these principles were pursued by Charles Darwin long ago, but they have not yet received sufficient attention from the ethnologists. Regarding biological classification, Darwin says, "The classification is not arbitrary like the grouping of the stars in constellations. . . . No doubt organic beings, like all other objects, can be classed in many ways, either artificially by single characters, or more naturally by a number of characters. We know, for instance, that minerals and the elemental substances can be thus arranged. In this case there is of course no relation to genealogical succession, and no cause can at present be assigned for their falling into groups."

Darwin was willing to concede that the previous effort made towards classification was not entirely useless. The biologists were classifying their material by what they called the *natural system*. They were unconsciously following the principle of descent. They laid stress on the relative permanence of the various characteristics, and the habit of attaching importance to those parts which were of highest importance to the very life of the organism had fallen into disrepute. But nobody else, besides Darwin, had brought the fact into prominence, "that the mere physiological importance of an organ does not determine its classificatory value." He says, "Numerous instances could be given of characters derived from parts which must be considered of very trifling physiological importance, but which are universally admitted as highly serviceable in the definition of whole groups. . . . The importance, for classification, of trifling characters, mainly depends on their being correlated with many other characters of more or less importance. The value of an aggregate of characters is very evident in natural history." Darwin correctly observed that in the classification of species, when the scientists use what they call the "natural system," they do nothing but classify them according to the principle of descent. He observed that the classification according to the geographical distribution is not logical. Regarding the classification of varieties in his day he expressed his opinion that it had been almost arbitrary. Regarding the unconscious acceptance of the principle of descent by the biologists, he says that "the characters which naturalists consider as showing true affinity between any two or more species, are those which have been inherited from a common parent, all true classification being genealogical; that community of descent is the hidden bond which naturalists have been unconsciously seeking, and not some unknown plan of creation, or the enunciation of general propositions, and the mere putting together and separating objects more or less alike."

Darwin has also given us valuable comments regarding the anthropological classification. He took illustrations from the science of languages in order to illustrate the principles of biological classifications. He says, "If we possessed a perfect pedigree of mankind, a genealogical arrangement of the races of man would afford the best classification of the various languages now spoken throughout the world; and if all extinct languages, and all intermediate and slowly changing dialects, were to be included, such an arrangement would be the only possible one. Yet it might be that some ancient languages had altered very little and had given rise to few new languages, whilst others had altered much owing to the spreading, isolation, and state of civilization of the several co-descended races, and had thus given rise to many new dialects and languages. The various degrees of difference between the languages of the same stock, would have to be expressed by groups subordinate to groups; but the proper or even only possible arrangement would still be genealogical; and this would be strictly natural, as it would connect together all languages, extinct and recent, by the closest affinities, and would give the filiation and origin of each tongue."

The experience of the biologists and the anthropologists has been somewhat similar. Both classes of students started in the same manner. They gathered the data and tried to classify it in the manner which they thought best, and when they found different principles with which they could classify the data, they began to quarrel among themselves, each regarding the principles of their schools as superior to those of the other. But the anthropologists did not start without any preconception in the study of the material, as the biologists had to do. The anthropologists, when they started in their study, had the biblical theories regarding the specific unity of mankind, and of the threefold division of the human race, namely, Semitic, Hamitic and Japhetic. And with the progress of knowledge when they found races speaking Aryan languages, but did not find the Japhetic races, they tried to identify the "Aryans" with the Japhetic races.

Some of the students of anthropology who tried to divorce themselves from the old biblical theory advocated the same principle which Comte had done; that is, they preferred to study the material by itself in the form of various human races spread all over the world, various human languages, various superstitions and folk-lores and other phases of civilization. The foundation is also laid down for anthropometry. And by the pursuit of this method they gathered a large amount of data and tried to classify human races in their light. The discussion regarding the comparative value of the languages of the anthropometric data on one hand and of linguistic affinities and folk-lore, etc., on the other, has not ended.

They ask "What is the test of the race? Is it the language or physical features or customs?"

If we take the word race to mean a collection of people with common descent, to the above question I should reply thus: There is no single test of race (descent) which would be universally applicable. Physical similarity and dissimilarity, customs, languages and many other characteristics of men as well as of societies are capable of change and decay. In fact, the desire of seeking easy solutions with universally applicable principles has done much towards creating confusion in science. The inquiry in this science should not start by the classification of existing human species in the light of one single secondary principle like complexion, hair-section or language, but the history of the present and past races of mankind needs to be constructed laboriously, giving each of the various criteria their due according to the scientific laws of evidence. Classification, itself, should not be regarded as the aim of anthropology, but only as means to construct the complete system of human genealogy. We should start with the existing tribes and see whether any of the present tribes are products of one pre-existing tribe. We should then take such pre-existing tribes and see whether any two of these pre-existing tribes are descended from one tribe of a more remote period. We should also see whether any of the present tribes is a product of two or more tribes, and if we find it to be the case, the descent of all the component tribes should be sought for. Carrying this process to its logical extent, we should be able to acquire the knowledge of the entire history of the development of the known races from one or more pre-existing anthropoid species according as the monogenic or polygenic doctrine be true.

When we wish to make a research of this kind, we should have a provisional theory regarding human progress, and should direct the researches to test that theory. A theory that appears to be unconsciously adopted by sociologists and anthropologists in their investigations appears to be as follows—

Mankind has evolved at a certain place and at a certain period from a pre-existing anthropoid form.

The number of human beings on earth has grown constantly during the last several thousand years of man's life. It grew from a few thousands at the most to about fifteen hundred millions. During the earlier stages of human culture, mankind was becoming separated into larger numbers of communities by the migration of its members. During such separations the separated groups became greatly, though never completely, isolated.

During later stages the groups are showing a constant tendency towards communication, association, federation and intermixture.

Man is migrating in search of his maintenance. He stops at a certain place, indefinitely at certain times. This stoppage depends on his appreciation of the resources of the place. This appreciation depends on the state of civilization he is in. It also determines his future civilization.

During the period of separation, the physical and linguistic differences multiplied, and thus various and numerous races have evolved. During the period of communication, confederation and intermixture, these differences are tending to be minimized.

The separation and isolation of social groups is breaking up by communication and by the formation of larger social units.

Consciousness of larger social units has come into existence through various causes. "Missionary religions" and the formation of larger political bodies are the chief of them.

Larger political bodies come into existence by the federation of tribes or states.

This federation comes into existence in various ways, one tribe conquers another and absorbs her. Sometimes one strong nation conquers a number of other nations and imposes on them a unity; sometimes several small states unite in fear of a huge enemy.

Printed by Butler & Tanner *Frome and London.*